14 NOV 2009

T

/S

; Guide

Soft Toys

A Collector's Guide

Frankie Leibe

Special Consultants:
Leyla Maniera
Daniel Agnew

MILLER'S SOFT TOYS: A COLLECTOR'S GUIDE
by Frankie Leibe
Special Consultants: Leyla Maniera and Daniel Agnew

FOR OUR MOTHERS

First published in Great Britain in 2000 by Miller's, a division of
Mitchell Beazley, imprints of Octopus Publishing Group Ltd,
2–4 Heron Quays, London E14 4JP

Miller's is a registered trademark of Octopus Publishing Group Ltd

Commissioning Editor **Liz Stubbs**
Executive Art Editor **Vivienne Brar**
Project Editor **Clare Peel**
Designer **Louise Griffiths**
Picture Research **Jenny Faithfull**
Production **Nancy Roberts**
Indexer **Sue Farr**
Jacket photography **Steve Tanner**

The publishers will be grateful for any information that will assist
them in keeping future editions up to date. Although all reasonable
care has been taken in the preparation of this book, neither the
publishers nor the compilers can accept any liability for any
consequence arising from the use thereof, or the information
contained therein.

ISBN 1 84000 185 2
A CIP catalogue record for this book is available from the
British Library
Set in Bembo, Frutiger and Shannon
Produced by Toppan Printing Co., (HK) Ltd.
Printed and bound in China

Jacket (left to right): "Beaky Baa" by Einco, c.1918;
"Dismal Desmond" by Dean's, 1928; "Big Bad Wolf"
by Schuco, 1950s; "Peter Rabbit" by Steiff, c.1908

contents

Where to start

Soft toys, as opposed to the headline-grabbing teddy bears of recent years, are a comparatively recent fun and affordable collecting area. Academic research on the subject is still in its infancy; extensive museum collections are rare, and there are very few specialist reference books. So how and where should the novice collector begin? The best place is with the toys themselves. What you collect will depend first and foremost on what you like, and secondly on your budget. Very early toys (pre-World War I) are rare – few were made; many were destroyed for reasons of hygiene after their owners' childhood illnesses; many were discarded as their owners outgrew them and any that have survived in good condition will be very expensive as they are now also of historical interest. There is, however, a huge variety of much less expensive post-World War I and II toys to choose from. Some people collect by type – dogs, cats, bears (very popular) or cartoon characters (across the board, Disney, or just Bonzo or Felix); some, like Steiff aficionados, collect by manufacturer. There are musical toys, mechanical toys, mascots, novelties and miniatures – the permutations are endless.

Whatever you decide to collect, try to buy the very best you can afford. Toys of good quality and condition nearly always keep their

value and will allow you to trade up, as and when your expertise grows and your tastes change. Soft toys, in particular, are an area where handling is the best way to acquire the experience that gradually builds up to expertise. A friendly local dealer is your best ally: here you may be able to handle a wide range of toys and learn to "feel" the difference between the various stuffings, fabrics, types of eyes and joints. Try to visit dolls and antique-toy fairs and specialist auctions; spend time at the viewing, using the catalogue to help you learn the differences between the manufacturers so that you may, eventually, be able to identify

unmarked toys. Don't be afraid to ask questions; most enthusiasts love to share their knowledge.

When you see a toy you like, pick it up: feel it to identify the fabric (see p.27); squeeze it to identify the stuffing; check the eyes; if dressed, take off the clothes to check overall condition and look for a mark, label or button to identify the manufacturer and age. If you buy from a dealer, ask for a receipt that includes details of condition, age and manufacturer (if known).

Even with a very limited budget it will be possible to build up a collection. There really are unexpected bargains to be found in car-boot sales and charity shops. Few collections will be valuable enough to warrant separate insurance or pose security risks, but photograph your toys and record where and when you bought them and how much they cost. Unless your penchant is for large pull-along toys or studio pieces, display won't be a problem, and care and restoration are largely common sense (see p.60). The major problem for most collectors is their inability to resist the "ah" factor – the very quality that attracted them in the first place. Don't be afraid of making mistakes – you will learn from them. If, in spite of all your resolutions, you fall in love with a toy, buy it, whatever the condition. It may be possible to restore it, but even if you can't the pleasure it gives you will sustain you on the endless but thoroughly enjoyable hunt for that elusive perfect toy that might just be round the corner.

Prices & dimensions
Prices for toys vary, depending on condition. The prices given throughout this book are for toys in fair to excellent condition and should be seen as guides to value only.

Abbreviations used for dimensions are as follows: **ht** height; **l.** length; **w.** width. Dimensions are given in centimetres and inches.

History

The interest in soft toys as a collecting area gathered momentum in the 1980s, some 100 years after Margarete Steiff produced her first homemade felt elephant pincushions as presents for her family and friends (see p.56). Although homemade soft toys had been produced from scraps of old fabric and animal skins for centuries, Steiff remains the earliest documented manufacturer, having applied in 1892 for a patent to make "animals and other figures to serve as playthings". The toys were initially overshadowed by the success of bears, launched in 1903 at the Leipzig Toy Fair, where a far-sighted buyer realized the potential of the "stuffed misfits", ordered 3,000 and began the passion for teddy bears that was to make the name Steiff famous. The innovatory modern glass factory in Giengen (see below, c.1910) flourished.

Inspired by the success of the Steiff bears, other companies began to make soft toys: in Germany, Gebrüder Bing, one of the best known of all toy manufacturers, produced soft

toys from c.1907, Schuco (see p.31) from c.1910. In Britain, Farnell produced bears (including the original Winnie-the-Pooh, see p.7) and soft toys from c.1908; Dean's Rag Book Co. produced from c.1910, and Chad Valley and Chiltern from c.1915. Meanwhile, in the USA, the success of the "Teddy's Bear" produced by Morris Michtom launched the Ideal Novelty Toy Co. c.1903. The toys produced by these early companies, largely based on traditional pets and farmyard or zoo animals, were well modelled, usually in mohair, velvet or felt, and hand finished. Relatively small quantities, aimed at the higher end of the market, were made.

After World War I the influence of Hollywood and animated films, comic strips and cartoons gave rise to a new generation of soft toys based on popular characters, and small sophisticated "novelty" toys that reflected the frenetic and fun-loving years of the 1920s and 1930s were also created. Department stores such as Hamleys, in

London, included favourites such as "Flip the Frog" and "Mickey Mouse" in their ranges, as shown in the illustration above of a page from Hamleys' late 1920s catalogue. Licensing and merchandizing flourished, and manufacturers competed fiercely for the growing market.

World War II brought production virtually to a halt; toys were a low priority, so homemade ones, like the "sow" and "piglets" below, came to the fore again. Production was slow to revive after the war, and a shortage of natural materials and a depressed economy resulted in the increasing use of cheaper manmade fibres and plastic. Greater stress on hygiene and safety standards also dictated materials and the fixing of eyes, noses etc. In Britain small companies, such as Wendy Boston, entered the field, while large established companies, such as Steiff and Farnell, were, in the late 1950s and early 1960s, challenged by Japanese manufacturers, who began mass-production of "cheap and cheerful" soft toys, often directly based on European and American models. Toys were, as ever, inspired by historical events, with television providing an increasing source of inspiration. In the 1960s, 1970s and 1980s, mass-production, mass-marketing and the virtually exclusive use of manmade fibres resulted in toys that were less well modelled, often garishly coloured and of ephemeral fashion-led designs. Ironically, it was at this time that soft toys emerged as a collecting area. Manufacturers were quick to capitalize on the trend, and in the late 20thC companies began to issue high-quality limited editions of replicas of their early 20thC toys, this time aimed at the collectors.

Dogs

The unique status of the dog as "man's best friend" is reflected in the large numbers produced as soft toys. All manufacturers made dogs and competed fiercely for sales with new lines, ranging from the fashionable dog of the moment – the French bulldogs of the 1920s and 1930s or the latest winner at Cruft's dog show – to well-known characters – Nipper the HMV dog or Rin-tin-tin – as well as novelties, mascots and promotional material. The huge quantity means that dogs are readily found and often inexpensive. A known maker and/or the presence of manufacturers' marks or labels will add to value, and, in general, pre-war dogs are of better quality and more sought after than later examples.

▼ **"Bully" by Steiff**

A French bulldog was the ultimate fashion accessory in chic society in the 1920s and 1930s. In 1927 Steiff capitalized on this by registering "Bully", and over 250,000 toy bulldogs were sold in the first five years of production. "Bully" appeared as a pincushion, a handbag and even a gramophone record cleaner in addition to the soft toy, which also came in a standing version, a ride-on and a pull-along toy. The huge ears were often stiffened with wire so that they could be bent into different positions. Made in sizes from 10cm to 51cm (4–20in), in various colours with glass eyes, this popular toy was made into the 1960s, although pre-World War II examples are most valuable.

"Bully" by Steiff, 1920s,
ht 41cm/16in, **£200–800**

"Tige" by Steiff,
c.1914,
ht 25.5cm/10in,
£100–300

◀ **"Tige" by Steiff**

"Tige" was modelled on the Boston bull-terrier owned by the cartoon character Buster Brown, who was created in 1906 by R.F. Outcault and featured in the *New York Herald*. Steiff patented their "Tige" design in 1912 and produced it in three sizes (18cm/7in, 23cm/9in and 28cm/11in), in either brown mohair or brown burlap (shown here), with "googly" glass eyes or black boot-button eyes, and with a squeaker or growler in the tummy. Ribbons and the real leather muzzle were an optional extra, but all Steiff "Tiges" have fully jointed bodies, the delightful expression seen here and superb modelling.

"Waldi" by Steiff, 1950s,
ht 23cm/9in, **£80–150**

▲ **"Waldi" by Steiff**
Dachshunds in different sizes
and poses, dressed and
undressed, were produced by
Steiff from 1937 until 1941,
when World War II stopped
production. It resumed in
the 1950s, and post-war
dachshunds can be identified
by the cursive script used
on the Steiff button (see p.59).
This particular "Waldi" has
mohair hands, feet and head,
but a cotton body underneath
his smart hunting outfit – a
green felt suit and hat and
a cotton checked shirt. He
is in excellent condition and
comes complete with all his
accessories, including his
wooden gun and a hat
secured by a stitch – both
rarely found still in place.

▼ **"Caesar" by Bing**
Caesar, the favourite pet of
Edward VII, endeared himself
to the public when, unleashed,
he followed his master's coffin.
Caesar was reproduced by
manufacturers including the
German company Gebrüder
Bing, who issued him as part
of their "Trippel-Trappel" range
of moving toys. This "Caesar"
still has his original leather
collar complete with name tag
stating "I am Caesar" on the
front and with the initials
"GBN" (Gebrüder Bing
Nürnberg) on the back.

"Trippel-Trappel" Caesar by Bing,
1920s, ht 23cm/9in, **£100–300**

"Caesar" by Farnell, 1920s,
ht 10cm/4in, **£40–100**

▲ **"Caesar" by Farnell**
Farnell's "Caesar" was
produced in many sizes
in black and white mohair
stuffed with wood wool. The
smaller, less expensive dogs
had pinned joints; larger
versions had wooden disc
joints. Farnell "Caesars" have
been found with their original
swing-tag labels, or with
remnants of white cotton on
the chest where the label
has been removed.

English Airedale, 1910–20s,
ht 33cm/13in, **£60–200**

▲ **English Airedale**
Everything about this Airedale
spells quality: it is well
modelled, with a good dense
mohair coat in two colours,
it has its original studded
leather collar, and, although
it is unjointed, its wood wool
stuffing is still sufficiently
strong to maintain the
characteristically alert terrier
pose, right down to its jaunty
feet. Although the excellent
condition and quality make
this dog eminently collectable,
it has no manufacturer's label
(often found sewn between
a dog's legs) and cannot
be attributed with certainty.
Nevertheless, the typically
"English" glass eyes (see p.39)
and overall quality suggest
that it was probably made
by Farnell or Chiltern.

Cycle mascot by Schuco, 1920s–
30s, ht 12.5cm/5in, **£100–400**

▲ **Cycle mascot by Schuco**
Schuco (see p.31) was well
known for its clockwork toys,
and many of its soft toys
were derived from tinplate
prototypes. This little dog is
a very rare cycle mascot: the
metal clip between the legs
allows it to be clipped to the
handlebars and carries the
name of the bicycle maker
who commissioned it. The
fully jointed metal frame is
covered with long mohair
fabric. The cut-glass eyes are
backed with silver foil and
may have been intended to
act as mini-reflectors.

"Mascot" dog by Schuco,
1955–65, ht 7.5cm/3in, **£40–80**

▲ **"Mascot" dog by Schuco**
Many Schuco mascots were
produced as inexpensive
novelties, and their small size
has made them appealing,
both then and now. This dog
has the typical Schuco metal-
frame head and body, but its
arms and legs are made from
mohair-covered wire. The
delightful German costume
is glued on, although the
slippers come off to reveal
very rudimentary looped
metal feet. Rabbits, mice and
cats were all part of the range,
which is comparatively rare in
Britain but relatively readily
found in continental Europe.
Any "Mascot" toy needs to
have all its accessories to fetch
its maximum value.

Wood wool

Thin wood shavings, known as wood wool or excelsior, were used predominantly to stuff pre-war toys. When squeezed it has a hard "crunchy" feel and crackly sound, and if it is in good condition will spring back. It is susceptible to damp, which causes loss of body and tone.

"Noah's Ark" poodle by Schuco, late 1950s, ht 5.5cm/2¼in, **£40–150**

▲ "Noah's Ark" poodle by Schuco

The popular "Noah's Ark" miniatures included a range of creatures, from elephants and rabbits (both highly popular) to lions (see p.50) and ladybirds, all marketed in a distinctive box, as shown here. In spite of their tiny size, the animals were very well made, with fully jointed metal-frame bodies and rubber neck joint. This poodle is covered with curly mohair and has a stitched nose and a tiny red felt tongue. The versions produced in synthetic material are less popular with collectors.

"Dismal Desmond" by Dean's, 1928, ht 28cm/11in, **£50–200**

▲ "Dismal Desmond" by Dean's

Dismal Desmond, the comic-strip character created by George Hildebrandt, was produced as a soft toy exclusively by Dean's Rag Book Co., in a huge variety of shapes, sizes and poses from 1923. Although "Desmond" was also produced in velveteen, the example seen here is made of pre-printed brushed cotton (still in exceptionally pristine condition) and includes the name "Dismal Desmond" (around the neck) and the Dean's registration number and logo. The unjointed body is well stuffed and modelled to produce a very engaging character who was more popular, and therefore produced in larger quantities and more readily found, than the rarer and less successful "Cheerful Desmond".

"Tatters the Hospital Pup" by Dean's, 1930, ht 24cm/9½in, **£100–300**

▲ "Tatters the Hospital Pup" by Dean's

"Tatters" may have been commissioned to promote a medical or hospital charity. Made by Dean's in pre-printed brushed cotton, he has plastic "googly" eyes and "tattered" ears sewn into the seams. His name and registration mark are printed on his neck. A comparatively rare dog, he is in excellent condition, which makes him very collectable.

▼ "Hot Stuff the Mustard Pup" by Chiltern

"Hot Stuff the Mustard Pup" was another promotional toy, commissioned from Chiltern by the Norwich-based Colman's Mustard Company. Colman's influenced the design, and the result was a tiny kapok-stuffed dog in mustard-coloured velvet, with airbrushed design, a rather strange moustache and a pink velvet nose. This example is in excellent condition and still has his original paper label, without which he would be totally anonymous. Small dogs are always popular with collectors, and this particular "Hot Stuff" is especially well made and very attractive.

"Hot Stuff the Mustard Pup" by Chiltern, 1920s, l. 7.5cm/3in, **£50–150**

▼ "Autograph Hound" by Merrythought

The major appeal of the "Autograph Hound" is his oddity. The long kapok-filled, cotton-covered body, with printed facial features, has been specially designed to provide space for as many autographs as possible. Although this dog is not particularly well modelled or made, his novelty appeal is enhanced by the presence of the original paper label that spells out his function: "Autograph Hound complete with ballpoint pen which will autograph all over hound's body, head and ears".

"Autograph Hound" by Merrythought, late 1950s/early 1960s, l. 46cm/18in, **£10–100**

▼ Japanese "Pepe"

Synthetic mohair-mix plush, increasingly commonly used from the 1950s, had become virtually universal by the 1970s. Whereas mohair mellows and improves with age, synthetic fabric tends to become matted and flattened and is generally less popular with collectors. This little synthetic plush dog, with plastic nose and eyes, is a good example of a post-war Japanese soft toy, but what makes this dog of particular interest to collectors is that he still has his original removable coat and paper label, both in excellent condition.

Japanese "Pepe", early 1960s, ht 13cm/5in, **£5–20**

▼ Scottie dog by Dean's

The Scottie dogs beloved of whisky manufacturers were also popular as ornaments and soft toys. This example, made by Dean's Rag Book Co., shows signs of the economy measures still in force after the war: it is less carefully modelled than many pre-war examples and has an unjointed stuffed body with weighted feet. The drooping head shows signs of wear, and the sewn-in ears have not been seamed at the ends. The original tartan collar and harness are in place, but the lead has broken. The original cloth label is sewn into the underside. Although the dog's quality is lower than pre-war examples, this toy does have immense hang-dog charm.

Scottie dog by Dean's, mid-1940s, ht 27cm/ 10½in, **£15–50**

▼ English dog by Isa Toy

The slightly clumpy legs of this mohair dog conceal springs, which enable it to bounce gently when patted on the head or back. This "spring" feature was typically, but not exclusively, associated with the English manufacturer Isa Toy (whose original label appears on the dog's tummy) and was also used on other bears and ducks (see p.43). Although comparatively rare, this type of dog was neither as well modelled (note the floppy tail) nor as expensive as toys by better-known manufacturers, and will be correspondingly modestly priced.

English dog by Isa Toy, 1920s, ht 18cm/7in, **£20–60**

Types of stuffing

Many early toys were stuffed with the left-over scraps of material used to make them. Kapok – a lightweight, oily fibre from the silk-cotton tree – was used in toys after World War I. Light and soft, it could be firmly stuffed, and was often used with cotton, or velveteen. It is less vulnerable than wood wool but should never be made wet. Post-World War II, a variety of washable manmade stuffings were used.

▼ English comic dog

Made of mohair stuffed with wood wool, this unjointed and unmarked dog has an outsize head that gives it a typically "English" comic appeal. The large head is combined with swivel opaque glass eyes, which were accompanied by a label announcing "I turn my eyes" (see p.39). This dog was probably made as an inexpensive novelty; the rather grotesque design is typical of the 1920s and 1930s.

English comic dog, 1920s, ht 20cm/8in, **£20–60**

Cats

After dogs, cats have always been among the most popular household pets, and any child who could not have a real cat could at least have a toy one. There was less emphasis on breeds than with dogs, but soft-toy cats were realistically modelled (over-realistic cats can have a slightly sinister quality), "dressed", produced in the form of famous feline heroes – Dick Whittington's cat, Puss in Boots – as lucky black cats, or in comical or grotesque forms – as skittles, pull-alongs, musical toys, glove puppets and baby toys. Steiff as ever led the way, producing cats from 1897, but all manufacturers included cats in their ranges, and they are easy to find today.

Skittles by Steiff, c.1905, king pin ht 23cm/9in; other skittles ht 20.5/8in; set **£1,000 –4,000**; individual skittles **£100–300 each**

▲ Skittles by Steiff

Sets of Steiff skittles often included just one cat among a range of animals, with a bear king pin (see p.57), so this very rare and valuable all-cat set was probably a special order. It was made for the European market (American skittles have 10 pieces rather than nine) and would have come with a felt ball (now missing). Made in either felt (as here) or velvet on turned wooden bases, skittles can be collected as individual pieces as well as sets.

▼ Wheeled cat by Steiff

Black cats were often intended for the English market, where they were considered lucky, as was probably the case with this pull-along black burlap cat on metal spoked wheels. The sturdy wire frame used for Steiff pull-along and ride-on toys was remarkably strong – an advertisement showed an adult standing straddled on the back of two wheeled toys. Although the Steiff button is missing, this cat can be identified both from Steiff catalogues and from its high quality and modelling.

Wheeled cat by Steiff, 1905–10, ht 33cm/13in, **£300–800**

"Puss in Boots" by Steiff, *c.*1912, ht 51cm/20in, **£600–2,500**

▲ "Puss in Boots" by Steiff

Steiff registered this "Puss in Boots" design in 1911 and produced it in three sizes. This was a luxury toy, made of very good quality mohair with a fully jointed body and a delightful costume – a magnificent felt hat with plume, a ruff and a yellow sash, originally marked "Steiff". However, the pièce de résistance is the felt-and-leather boots that cover the unmodelled feet. This example is in excellent condition and is only missing a wooden sword.

"Throw" cat by Steiff, c.1910, ht 23cm/9in, **£300–1,200**

▲ "Throw" cat by Steiff

"Throw" dolls were a Steiff range, now rare, produced for very young children. The soft felt cylinder-shaped stuffed bodies, with "mama" voice boxes, had jointed heads, with simply made mohair arms and legs sewn on. This little cat is wearing her original cotton dress and has a Steiff button in her ear. She also carries a retailer's label on her base that tells us she was made for Charles Morrell, who owned three famous toy shops in London from 1870 until 1916.

▼ "Puss in Boots" by Kersa

Soft toys produced by Kersa were usually made of felt (see p.27), but this "Puss in Boots" is in black-and-white mohair, with striking red boots. The white glass eyes are also atypical. His neck ribbon is probably a later replacement, but he has great charm, even though he lacks the high Steiff quality, and he would be far more modestly priced. Kersa toys are usually marked with a square metal button (now often missing) on the foot.

"Puss in Boots" by Kersa, 1950s, ht 25.5cm/10in, **£60–120**

Musical cat by Farnell, 1930s,
ht 30.5cm/12in, **£60–200**

▲ Musical cat by Farnell

The English company Farnell
also produced a range of toys
under the Alpha tradename.
The mechanism – probably
Swiss – used in this Alpha cat
was similar to that used in a
musical box and was activated
by winding with a brass key;
the winding hole is usually
on the underside of the toy.
These musical toys are keenly
collected but should always be
in working order and good
condition. This realistically
modelled cat, with its dense
black mohair coat and original
label, is a great example.

Musical cat by Jopi, 1920s,
ht 36cm/14in, **£80–200**

▲ Musical cat by Jopi

Although unmarked, this cat
is typical of the musical soft
toys made by the German
company Jopi. The musical
device played a tune and was
activated by squeezing the
cat's stomach several times;
evidence of use can be seen
in the slight flattening at
the sides of the lovely long
mohair tabby marked coat.
This cat is in excellent
condition, with typical Jopi
orange, rather staring eyes
and velvet-lined ears, and still
has its original bell.

Dressed musical cat by Farnell,
1930s, ht 30.5cm/12in, **£100–300**

▲ Dressed musical cat
by Farnell

This little dressed cat, made of
artificial silk plush, is another
of Farnell's musical toys. Here,
however, there is no attempt
at realistic modelling: the cat
sits on rudimentary back legs,
with jointed head and arms,
dressed in its original pale
pink silky bonnet and bolero.
Although unmarked, this toy
has been identified from
similar known examples. Any
such light-coloured toys must
be in good clean condition,
as artificial silk plush is very
difficult to clean (see p.27).

FACT FILE

Musical toys
This is a very popular collecting niche. Good working condition is essential for high value, as repair, replacement or restoration of a musical movement is expensive. Many musical toys have fixed keys; a missing key is rarely a problem, as other clockwork, or clock, keys often fit.

"Fifi" by Einco, 1912, ht 23cm/9in, **£60–200**

▲ **"Fifi" by Einco**
Both Farnell and Chiltern made toys for Eisenmann & Co., a major toy distributor and importer whose director, Joseph Eisenmann, was known as the King of the Toy Trade before World War I. "Fifi" was marketed under Einco's "Kiddieland" trademark, registered in 1911 (see p.58), and has the characteristic swivel eyes, together with the original swing tag carrying her name and the words "I turn my eyes". This example is in exceptionally good condition and is highly sought after, as is the "Tubby" dog in the same format.

"bigo-bello" cat by Schuco, 1950s, ht 33cm/13in, **£30–80**

▲ **"bigo-bello" cat by Schuco**
Part of the Schuco "bigo-bello" range (see p.31), this comic cat is a good example of a well-made 1950s toy whose sturdy construction has contributed to its continuing good condition. The wire armature is covered with mohair on the arms, legs, tail and head, but the clothed body is cotton – a common cost-saving feature on post-World War II toys. The only concession to realism is the green glass eyes, which have characteristic elliptical pupils.

"Mrs Twisty Puss" by Merrythought, 1965–7, ht 25.5cm/10in, **£30–80**

▲ **"Mrs Twisty Puss" by Merrythought**
"Mrs Twisty Puss" is one of a range of unjointed animals, including bears (very collectable) and dogs, made of a mohair-Dralon mix on a metal armature that could be "twisted" into many poses. Overenthusiastic "twisting" can weaken the structure, but this example is still in very good condition.

▼ Art Deco cat by Chad Valley

Bizarre stylized ceramic cats based on the humorous drawings of Louis Wain were very popular in the 1920s and 1930s, and their influence can be clearly seen in this Chad Valley Art Deco cat, with its bright green nose and mouth and eccentric "matchstick" eyes. The strangely shaped body is tightly stuffed and can only stand with difficulty. This is primarily an adult toy and will appeal equally to collectors of Art Deco and of cats. The Chad Valley label can be clearly seen on the foot.

Art Deco cat by Chad Valley, 1920s–30s, ht 25.5cm/10in, **£50–200**

▼ English "Roly Poly" cat

Steiff registered this type of "Roly Poly" toy in 1909, and this unmarked cat, although very similar in style, is almost certainly a copy. It is quite well made, but the weighted mohair body and jointed head, with padded, felt-lined ears, lack the quality and modelling of the Steiff toys. The glass eyes are typically "English", and this example may have been made by Farnell, possibly for only a short period as Steiff was swift to resort to the courts to protect its patented designs.

English "Roly Poly" cat, 1910, ht 16.5cm/6½in, **£80–300**

▼ Cat by Wendy Boston

The company established by Wendy Boston in 1945 pioneered safety eyes and washable toys in the late 1950s. Its soft toys were less successful than its bears, and cats are very unusual. This example is made of manmade fibre, with a printed velvet face, ears and paw pads. Wendy Boston toys are marked with cloth labels; they also have distinctive rounded bottoms with thin seams between the trunks and the legs that allow the toys to sit with their legs straight out in front, as seen here.

Cat by Wendy Boston, 1950s, ht 43cm/17in, **£20–60**

▼ Sailor cat by Merrythought

Some toys were made in small quantities, or as special orders for specific shops and retailers, as was possibly the case with this sailor cat. It is very well made and still in good condition, with a jointed freestanding mohair body dressed in fine clothes – cotton trousers and a delightful jacket with piping and braiding, topped by a smart sailor's cap. The printed label dates it to the 1930s, as do the inset glass eyes that were used on earlier Merrythought toys.

Sailor cat by Merrythought, 1930s, ht 29cm/11½in, **£100–300**

Unmarked toys

Many toys are unmarked, sometimes because they were never marked in the first place (true with many small makers), because parents removed labels for saftey reasons, or because the tag has simply become detached. A marked toy will always have more appeal to a collector, but unmarked toys will be cheaper and may be identified later from retailers' or company catalogues, or other marked examples or by features associated with certain companies.

▼ Cat by Dean's

This unusual soft filled cat by Dean's Rag Book Co. was originally covered in bells, only two of which are still in place. It may well have been intended for a young baby, who would have enjoyed the sound it made as an adult shook it; or, with its green plastic "googly" eyes and red velvet tunic top (the distinctive Dean's label is sewn under the collar), it may have been intended as a court jester.

Cat by Dean's, 1930s, ht 41cm/16in, **£50–150**

▼ English cat

Little is known about this unmarked tiny cat. Fully jointed, it is made of English mohair (now rather faded), with a printed velvet face on which the remains of the features and a big smile are just visible. However, the well-shaped stitched toes and claws are still clearly marked. This example may have been designed as an adult novelty rather than a child's toy. It has great appeal, and its uncertain origin may well be clarified when and if a marked similar toy appears on the market.

English cat, 1920s, ht 11.5cm/4½in, **£40–140**

Rabbits

Rabbits are second only to elephants in terms of popularity with collectors. Although rabbit skins may have been used to make early toys, soft-toy rabbits first appeared in the Steiff catalogue in 1897, when records detail sales of 1,088 rabbits in one year (compared with 1,215 elephants), and were subsequently produced by all manufacturers. Early rabbits tended to be realistically modelled and appeared as pincushions, babies' rattles and skittles as well as in the guise of such characters as Peter Rabbit and Jack Rabbit, from popular children's books, and variations on the ever-popular Easter Bunny. Values with depend on condition and rarity; pre–World War II rabbits are most sought after, but that inimitable "ah" factor will ultimately determine collectability.

▼ **"Peter Rabbit" by Steiff**

Peter Rabbit, possibly one of the best-loved soft toys ever made (see p.57), was produced under licence by Steiff from 1905. He was made first in velvet and then also in the rarer and more sought-after white lamb plush shown here. The little felt jacket (usually blue; red is rare) and slippers (invariably red) with leather soles are removable and are often missing. This charming example is in complete untouched condition and has all his accessories, which enhances his appeal and value.

"Peter Rabbit" by Steiff, c.1908, ht 20cm/8in, **£500–2,000**

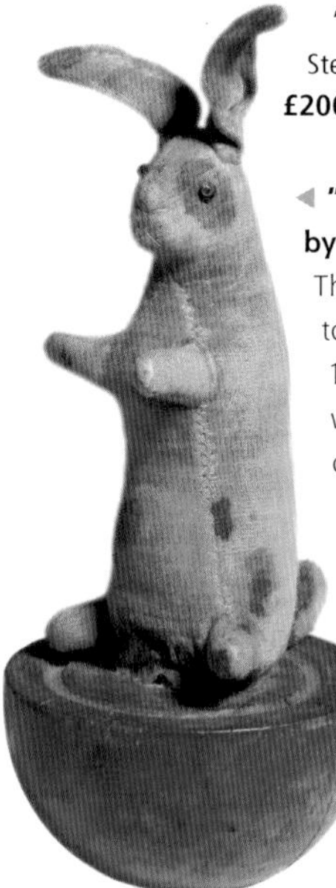

"Roly Poly" rabbit by Steiff, c.1900, ht 12.5cm/5in, **£200–600**

◄ **"Roly Poly" rabbit by Steiff**

The Steiff "Roly Poly" toys launched in the 1890s were fixed to wooden bases and were designed to wobble but not topple over. They were made as sets and individually and came in a variety of animal forms, including cats, elephants and dogs. This velvet rabbit is faded, and its base cracked, but its age and rarity compensate for its well-played-with condition. Made before Steiff introduced the ear button, it can be identified from catalogues.

FACT FILE

Famous rabbits

When *The Tale of Peter Rabbit* was published in 1902, Beatrix Potter made her own doll but could not find an English manufacturer, so in 1905 Steiff took up the option. Steiff also produced "Jack Rabbit", the hero of *Jack Rabbit's Adventures* by Dave Cory, published by Grosset & Dunlap in New York.

▼ **Baby's rattle by Steiff**

This tiny little rabbit, made of soft velvet with painted markings, was produced as a baby's rattle. Unjointed, and stuffed with a soft filling that encloses the rattle, it is in exceptionally good condition, with what are probably its original ribbon and bell. Miniatures are always popular, and these tiny rattles, made also in the form of elephants and bears, display the same high quality, attention to detail and modelling that are the hallmarks of all Steiff toys.

Baby's rattle by Steiff, *c.*1900, ht 9cm/3½in, **£50–400**

"Holland" rabbit by Steiff, *c.*1913, ht 20cm/8in, **£80–300**

▲ **"Holland" rabbit by Steiff**

The "Holland" rabbit was the brainchild of Franz Steiff, Margarete Steiff's nephew. He developed the ball-and-socket jointed ears with their realistic movement, launched in 1908, which were used on a whole range of animals and swiftly copied by manufacturers around the world. Made of mohair, with jointed limbs, head and ears, the "Holland" rabbit is a good example of the fine modelling used for early Steiff toys. Although slightly worn, this example is in excellent condition for such an early toy. He would have been expensive to make, and has kept both his high quality and its value.

"Jack Rabbit" by Steiff, 1927–31, ht 28cm/11in, **£600–3,000**

▲ **"Jack Rabbit" by Steiff**

Steiff manufactured "Jack Rabbit" under licence from 1927 to 1931, producing 2,780 dolls in two sizes (23cm/9in and 28cm/11in) for export to the USA. "Jack Rabbit" is now extremely rare; this example, in superb condition, complete with lollipop, is held in the extensive Steiff archives.

▼ Little girl rabbit by Steiff

This charming little girl rabbit illustrates the gradual move away from realistically modelled rabbits towards a more doll-like dressed novelty toy. Made of golden mohair and fully jointed, it can be posed in different positions, including standing on its card-reinforced feet. The removable dress is original and can be identified as such from the Steiff catalogue; there was also a little boy rabbit with shorts. Original clothes are rare; some rabbits have been redressed, and later examples have fixed clothes.

Little girl rabbit by Steiff, 1930s, ht 23cm/9in, **£100–400**

▼ "Master Bunny" by Farnell

"Master Bunny" was one of the early pre-World War I Alpha soft toys made by Farnell, and his somewhat crude modelling and stuffed unjointed body provide an interesting contrast with early Steiff rabbits. Such toys would have been modestly priced: only the head, ears and tips of the paws were mohair, and the fixed clothes formed the body. This particular "Master Bunny", who closely resembles contemporary Einco/Chiltern toys, has his original swing-tag label and is an interesting, quirky and rare example of an early English soft toy.

"Master Bunny" by Farnell, c.1914, ht 20cm/8in, **£80–300**

▼ Dressed rabbit by Chiltern

This little rabbit was probably inspired by the success of the Steiff dressed toys. It has a mohair head, legs and paws and stands on solid flat feet, the left one carrying a manufacturer's label on the base. Its cloth body is covered by original clothes, which add to the value – especially the presence of tiny accessories, such as the little flower seen here, that were so often lost.

Dressed rabbit by Chiltern, 1950s, ht 38cm/15in, **£100–250**

Dressed toys

Dressing animals added to their appeal and was a way of cutting down on the use of mohair, which was scarce after both World Wars. Removable clothes are often missing or replaced, but original accessories and clothes do add to value. Grubby clothes should be professionally cleaned.

FACT FILE

Pull-along rabbit by Chiltern, late 1950s, ht 18cm/7in, **£15–80**

"Skater" rabbit by Chiltern, 1920s, ht 30.5cm/12in, **£100–500**

▲ "Skater" rabbit by Chiltern

The fierce competition between manufacturers led to a never-ending search for novelty to generate new sales. Chiltern came up with the "Skater" rabbit – an unjointed toy with high-quality modelling. "Skater" was produced either in a mohair version, which was rarer and more expensive, or in the less highly priced and more readily found artificial silk plush. The clothes – a luxurious jacket (usually pink; green is rarer) with a white collar and matching white muff – are fixed. The example shown here is in top condition.

▲ Pull-along rabbit by Chiltern

Pull-along toys were a huge success and were produced in large quantities and in many different animal forms: the artificial-silk-plush rabbit shown here is even more interesting because it "pedals" its tricycle when it is pulled along. The near perfect condition of this rabbit – still brightly coloured, with an original ribbon and swing tag, which make the toy highly collectable – and the crucial factor that it came from unused shop stock, determine the value.

Rabbit by Chiltern, 1930s, ht 18cm/7in, **£100–400**

▲ Rabbit by Chiltern

This delightfully rotund rabbit is another example of unused shop stock. Made of brightly coloured artificial silk plush, with jointed arms and head but fixed legs, and stitched mouth and claws, it would have been quite inexpensive to make and is therefore modestly priced. What makes it of interest today is its superb condition.

"Rolly" rabbit by Schuco, 1950s, ht 23cm/9in, **£80–300**

"Easter Rabbit" by Kersa, after 1948, ht 23cm/9in, **£70–300**

Rabbit nightdress-case by Pixie Toys, 1930s, ht 65cm/25½in, **£40–150**

▲ **Rolly rabbit by Schuco**
Launched after World War II, Schuco's "Rolly" range of clockwork soft toys included monkeys, bears and clowns, as well as the rabbit shown here. The cloth body conceals metal legs; when wound up, the rabbit uses the stick to propel itself along on its skates. Such toys were expensive to produce and comparatively few were made. Although slightly faded, this rabbit is in perfect working order, which adds to both the overall appeal and the value. Any clockwork or mechanical toy should ideally be in working order, as repairs are costly and should only be carried out by a professional.

▲ **"Easter Rabbit" by Kersa**
Soft toys produced by short-lived companies are relatively scarce and keenly sought after by collectors who want to own an example from all known manufacturers. The Czech company Kersa, founded near Prague in 1920, moved in 1948 to Germany, where this charming little girl felt "Easter Rabbit" was made, together with a little boy "Easter Bunny". The little basket, which is removable and therefore rarely found, was probably orginally filled with Easter sweets. Although unmarked, this rabbit is attributable from other known examples and is still in particularly good condition.

▲ **Rabbit nightdress-case by Pixie Toys**
Initially established as a cottage industry in the early 1930s, Pixie Toys took off when Elizabeth Simmonds, who had worked for Merrythought and Norah Wellings, joined the company. This nightdress-case was inspired by her time at Merrythought, but the style of the rabbit, with its neat waist and full "skirts" in which the nightdress was stored, is influenced by Norah Wellings' designs. Although slightly faded, this nightdress-case still has its original label, a particular bonus with a product from such a little-known company, which eventually closed in 1962.

Materials

• **Mohair:** expensive, natural fabric used for good-quality toys (the more densely woven and longer it was, the more valuable the toy). To learn to distinguish different qualities and types, handle known examples until you can "feel" the difference. As a rough guide, German mohair is very densely woven, English mohair is densely woven, and some American mohair is very sparsely woven and quite bristly to the touch. To add to the confusion, all types of mohair were used by manufacturers of all nationalities. Although mohair ages well, once worn it cannot be restored.

• **Artificial silk plush:** manmade fibre with a characteristic shine and silky feel, used after World War I as a less expensive alternative to mohair. It was usually dyed and used to give the illusion of clothes. Light colours are often grubby and difficult to clean.

• **Felt:** wool cloth used for early toys and as inexpensive mohair substitute after World War II. Vulnerable to moths, it fades in sunlight and the colours will run drastically if it gets wet.

▼ English pot-holder rabbit

The English tradition of nursery life for young children generated a whole range of accessories, in particular furniture and ceramics, and this velvet rabbit would have been an inexpensive novelty – perhaps used for lifting the nursery teapot. It was probably unmarked from the beginning as there are no signs such as changes in colour, holes, thread to indicate a sewn-on label, and any tie-on tag has disappeared. It is, however, very similar to a range of velvet cats and dogs produced in the 1920s and 1930s by Farnell and Chad Valley.

English pot-holder rabbit, 1920s–30s, ht 13cm/5in, **£15–80**

▼ Rabbit by Chad Valley

Chad Valley, one of the most popular British soft toy manufacturers, began life as a printing company, producing its first soft toys – bears – in 1915; by 1938 the company was appointed Toymakers to Her Majesty the Queen. This green artificial-silk-plush rabbit, with large wire-framed ears and complete with squeaker, was made in the mid-1930s and is in superb mint condition, with original ribbon and embroidered label. It is an exceptional example of a rabbit by a popular English manufacturer.

Rabbit by Chad Valley, 1930s, ht 23cm/9in, **£30–90**

Monkeys & apes

Monkeys were popular in the late 19thC, when, possibly influenced by the theories of Charles Darwin, they were often produced as automata mimicking human behaviour, for example smoking cigarettes and drinking tea. Steiff produced soft-toy monkeys in 1892, and most manufacturers subsequently included monkeys in their ranges – realistically modelled, dressed and as a variety of mounted toys. However, in general, monkeys and apes are less popular with collectors than they are with children, and a monkey will need to be very unusual or in exceptional condition to attract attention and value. Less-expensive monkeys are readily found, often influenced by famous illustrators such as Clarence Lawson-Wood or by well-known monkey variety-show acts and the once popular chimps' tea-party.

▼ Monkey by Steiff
This early monkey has all the hallmarks of Steiff: good-quality mohair, a well-modelled, fully disc-jointed body, stitched-and-shaped fingers and toes and deep-set wooden boot-button eyes. The face has been modelled to make it as friendly and appealing as possible, which, together with its exceptional condition and early date, makes it very collectable; its predecessor – an early Steiff monkey with string joints – would be a unique find indeed.

Monkey by Steiff, c.1905, ht 56cm/22in, **£200–800**

▶ "Record Peter" by Steiff
"Record Peter" was a Steiff monkey on a self-drive chassis, with a squeaker in the seat, which was produced until the 1950s. Most "Record Peters" were simply plain brown; this unusual example is in black mohair with a coloured ruff. The felt face is very realistically modelled, with inset eyes, which make it more lifelike although slightly sinister. Brown "Record Peters" are often readily found and are marked with Steiff ear buttons (that help with dating), and the company name is also usually stamped on the wooden wheels.

"Record Peter" by Steiff, c.1910, ht 25.5cm/10in, **£150–500**

"Urpeter" by Steiff,
late 1920s, ht 20cm/8in,
£80–300

▲ "Urpeter" by Steiff

"Urpeter" was also a Steiff monkey on a chassis, in this case a clockwork metal one mounted on wooden wheels with an eccentric handlebar movement. The red/yellow colouring and teddy-bear motif were often used by Steiff, who produced this model from 1926 until 1929, together with a rare version with a bear, only 1,500 of which were made. Condition is critical to value; this example, with his pristine mohair and felt face with green glass eyes, will be very sought after.

▼ Mystery monkeys

Little is known about these monkeys. The use of stockinette for the somewhat grotesque features, which have been moulded and then painted, suggest they may be American in origin. Their unusually large size suggests that they may have been a special order, perhaps a promotional toy for one of the famous monkey variety acts popular in the 1920s, such as M. et Mme X, whom they closely resemble.

Mystery monkeys, c.1920s,
ht 66cm/26in, **£200–800**

Monkey by Berg, late 1950s/early 1960s, ht 11cm/4¼in, **£5–30**

▲ Monkey by Berg

This little mohair monkey was probably designed as an inexpensive dressing-table toy. It is primarily a fun toy, with a wire armature (a fully jointed version was also made) and a mohair body, and the plastic "googly" eyes found on many novelty toys. It was made by the German manufacturer Berg and has the distinctive metal-and-enamel heart trademark on its chest.

▼ "Tricky" orang-utan by Schuco

This delightful baby orang-utan, with bright unfaded orange mohair body, felt face, hands and feet and "yes/no" mechanism is part of Schuco's "Tricky" range, which consisted largely of bears and monkeys. When his tail is moved from left to right, he shakes his head; when the tail is moved up and down, he nods. The quality associated with Schuco shows in the careful modelling of the face – as with the Steiff monkey (see p.28), the stress is on charm and appeal – and in the inset glass eyes.

"Tricky" orang-utan by Schuco, 1950s, ht 25.5cm/10in, **£80–300**

▼ "Talisman" monkeys by Schuco

These tiny novelty monkeys, seen here with their original point-of-sale display box, were produced from the 1920s in huge quantities. Although inexpensive they were well made, with jointed metal bodies covered in mohair, tinplate face masks with tinplate eyes, and felt hands, feet and ears. Early examples have slightly textured painted faces; later examples have smooth glossy ones. They were produced in a whole range of colours – the more bizarre, the more collectable.

"Talisman" monkeys by Schuco, 1950s, ht 9cm/3½in, **£30–80** each

▼ Monkey lapel badge by Schuco

Schuco was very adept at marketing its novelties: the tiny metal-framed mohair-covered monkeys were produced in a whole range of forms, including the lapel badge shown here. An original Schuco pin is essential to value, and this pink lapel badge also has an original price tag. The brighter the colour – green, lavender, pink, red and blue versions were all produced – the more valuable the monkey, but it must be clean and unfaded. This example is slightly faded and grubby, which will considerably reduce its value.

Monkey lapel badge by Schuco, 1920s, ht 8cm/3¼in, **£60–150**

Schuco

Schuco (*see* p.59) was one of the most innovative of German toy manufacturers. Better known for its tinplate mechanical toys, it also made a popular range of miniature (5–11.5cm/ 2–4½in) soft toys from tinplate prototypes, with metal-frame jointed bodies covered in mohair and a tinplate face mask. These were made in novelty formats – powder compacts, scent bottles, lapel badges (opposite), mascots (*see* p.12) – all now highly collectable. Other desirable Schuco ranges: "Noah's Ark" (*see* pp.13, 50), "Rolly" (*see* p.26), "Tricky" (*see* opposite), "bigo-bello" (*see* p.19), "yes/no" mechanism toys (*see* opposite and p.50).

▼ Powder compact and lipstick by Schuco

Schuco miniature powder compacts and scent bottles were popular ladies' fashion accessories in the 1920s and 1930s. The body opened up to reveal the compact (an original powder puff will enhance the value), and the head pulled off to reveal a miniature lipstick or scent bottle. Both examples with lipsticks and those with scent bottles are keenly collected, with bears being particularly popular. This example is in very good condition, with bright red unfaded mohair.

Powder compact and lipstick by Schuco, 1920s/1930s, ht 9cm/3½in, **£70–300**

▼ Glove puppet by Schuco

The bell-hop associated with the smart hotels of the 1920s and 1930s was produced in many forms, including the monkey glove puppet shown here. Although glove puppets can be hard to display, they were (and still are) inexpensive and form an integral part of most soft-toy ranges. Few were marked, but this felt bell-hop puppet has the characteristic Schuco metal-framed mohair covered head with a metal face plate; many versions also came with a hat.

Glove puppet by Schuco, 1920s, ht 20cm/8in, **£50–200**

Disney characters

Soft toys based on the characters created by Walt Disney now form one of the most popular collecting areas. In the USA the first "Mickey" dolls (now extremely rare) were made from 1930 by Charlotte Clark, and by 1934 the Knickerbocker Toy Co. was producing both cuddly and standing versions of Disney characters. In Europe, licensed toys were made prior to World War II by Steiff and Dean's Rag Book Co., and by Merrythought and Schuco after the war. Mickey and Minnie remain firm favourites, and pre-war versions of them and other characters are the most keenly collected. In general, post-war toys tend to be less well made; however, the success of such films as *Winnie-the-Pooh and the Honey Tree* (1967) and *The Jungle Book* (1967) has provided collectors with a range of more readily available, affordable Disney soft toys.

"Mickey Mouse" by Steiff,
1930s, ht 43cm/17in,
£1,000–4,000

▶ **"Mickey Mouse"
by Steiff**
Disney created the character Mickey Mouse in 1928, and soft-toy versions were made by Steiff from 1931 until 1936. Smaller examples have painted facial features, but the larger toys, such as the felt-and-velveteen one shown here, have button eyes or applied-felt "cherry-pie" eyes. This example has the three-fingered hands typical of early versions, fixed card-lined feet, which enable him to stand, and, unusually, his tail. He is in fine condition, which, combined with his large size and the Steiff button in his ear, makes him very collectable.

▼ **"Pluto" by Schuco
and Japanese "Baloo"**
This mohair "Pluto" is part of the "bigo-bello" range of wire-framed high-quality soft toys by Schuco – one of the most collectable series of Disney characters made after World War II. Also manufactured after the war, but from the opposite end of the price and quality range, is this "Baloo" – an inexpensive, mass-produced Japanese synthetic-velvet toy, given away with tokens from cereal packets. However, he is in excellent condition and still complete with swing tag and side-seam label.

"Pluto" by
Schuco, 1950s,
ht 28cm/11in,
£100–400; "Baloo",
late 1950s, ht 16.5cm/
6½in, **£20–50**

▼ "Donald Duck" by Dean's

Although Donald Duck never enjoyed the superstar status of Mickey and Minnie Mouse, he was one of the next most popular characters. This mohair-and-felt version has a wire armature that allows him to be posed and stand on his own. The toy is in excellent condition, with clean, fluffy white mohair and brightly coloured felt with no moth damage. His original woven label under his sailor collar confirms that he was made in the late 1930s, not long after Dean's Rag Book Co. became the first British company to be granted the licence to produce Disney characters, in 1933.

"Donald Duck" by Dean's, late 1930s, ht 23cm/9in, **£100–400**

▼ "Pluto" by Dean's

"Pluto" was produced by several different American makers as well as Schuco and Merrythought in Europe, but in smaller quantities than many characters and is now fairly rarely found. This early example by Dean's is made of velveteen, pre-printed with facial features as well as the firm's registration mark and number round the neck. The wire armature (visible in the tail) has suffered from years of play: he has lost his ears, and the tail is just hanging on by a thread. Nevertheless, he can be restored, although poor condition will of course be reflected in the price.

"Pluto" by Dean's, 1930s, ht 10cm/4in, **£100–500**

- Licensed Disney toys are closely vetted and therefore truer to the original characters and more popular with collectors than unauthorized versions.
- Early Disney toys (1930s), especially those by Steiff, are generally better made and more desirable than the mass-made post-war examples.
- A Dean's "Mickey", or a lesser-known character, is a good starting-point.

▼ "Mickey Mouse" by Dean's

"Mickey Mouse" was launched by Dean's along with "Minnie Mouse" in 1933. This example has a velveteen body and head and flat hands – later versions have larger stuffed hands. Eyes were either shoe buttons (as here), metal or "googly". The buttoned shorts were usually red or blue, and invariably fixed or sewn on. Although the ink-stamp mark on the sole of the foot has usually worn off, the Dean's registration mark will be found printed around the neck of velveteen and brushed cotton toys. This version is slightly grubby (the face would usually be white), and his tail (always vulnerable) is missing.

"Mickey Mouse" by Dean's, c.1934, ht 18cm/7½in, **£80–400**

Comic characters

Comic characters inspired by cartoon strips, books, films and illustrators were produced in a wide range of formats, including soft toys. In general, the licensing of such characters was more relaxed than with Disney, and the charaacter of Felix the Cat, for example, who was so popular in the 1920s, appeared in many different styles, depending on whether he was manufactured in the USA, Britain or Germany. The firms of Chad Valley and Farnell led the way in Britain and produced many notable characters, some of whom, although highly popular at the time, are less sought after today; others, such as Bonzo and Winnie-the-Pooh's friends, have more than stood the test of time.

▼ **"Barney Googles" and "Spark Plug" by Steiff**
Barney Googles – the classic "little man" – was created by American cartoonist Billy De Beck for Hearst Newspapers in 1919; in 1922 Barney was given a racehorse – Spark Plug. They were made in tin, composition and, from 1925 until 1927, as felt and mohair soft toys by Steiff and are now very rare as only 613 were made. In addition to the Steiff button, the "Spark Plug" shown here also has a stamp on his back foot, reading "c.1924–5 King Feature Synd. Inc.".

"Barney Googles" and "Spark Plug" by Steiff, 1924–5, ht of "Barney Googles" 15cm/6in, ht of "Spark Plug" 18cm/8in, **£500–2,000**

▲ **"Bonzos" by Steiff**
Bonzo was created by the English illustrator G.E. Studdy in the 1920s and achieved instant popularity, which gave rise to a host of licensed products including games, tin toys and postcards. Steiff made some 115 fully jointed velvet prototypes, including a musical "Bonzo" (above, with yellow sash), none of which was approved and officially sold. Steiff "Bonzos", although extremely rare, are sometimes found. These examples, in excellent condition, are in the Steiff archive.

"Bonzo" prototypes by Steiff, 1920s, ht from 13cm/5in to 43cm/17in, **£1,000–6,000**

"Bonzo" by Chad Valley,
1920s, ht 11cm/4¼in, **£100–800**

▲ **"Bonzo" by Chad Valley**
Chad Valley was given UK
and worldwide Bonzo
licensing rights and produced
him in great quantities from
approximately the mid-1920s
to the mid-1930s in a wide
variety of different sizes
and styles, including
one with a dummy.
Although "Bonzos"
are sought after –
even in poor
condition – this
particular example,
with an airbrushed
velvet body and
jointed head, is
in perfect, mint
condition. He has a
charming moulded face
with painted eyes and is
complete with his original
leather collar, swing tag,
celluloid-covered metal
button and white-and-red
woven label on one foot.

▼ **"Tim Tale" by Chad Valley**
Chad Valley also produced
"Tim Tale", a comic character
who appeared in the *Daily
Mail* in the 1930s. "Tim Tale"
is quite rare, especially in the
good condition seen here,
where he still sports the blue-
red-and-gold label also found
on Chad Valley bears and
a badge on his felt jacket
embroidered with his initials
and the words "Daily Mail".
His felt outfit is clean, with no
moth damage, and his velvet
head (with painted eyes), ears
and hands are all immaculate;
this adds greatly not only to
his visual appeal but also
to his value.

"Tim Tale" by Chad Valley, 1930s,
ht 29cm/11½in, **£80–300**

Mystery felt
mouse, late 1950s,
ht 33cm/13in,
£60–200

• Comic characters are
now among the most
sought-after soft toys.
They often appeal to
early animation
enthusiasts (*see* p.37).
• Bonzo and Felix the
Cat are niche collecting
areas in their own right.
• Some characters –
Steiff's "Spark Plug",
"Bonzo" and his
girlfriend "Oola" and
"Bertha the Siberian
Cheesehound" (*see* p.55)
– were made in small
quantities and are rare.
• "Disneyana"(*see* pp.
32–3) is a popular niche.

▼ **Mystery felt mouse**
In the 1950s Spanish
and Italian manufacturers
produced several versions
of comic dressed felt mice.
This seems to be a version
of Topo Gigio – a popular
Italian character created by
Maria Perego in an outfit
that was perhaps inspired
by the Mouseketeers of *Tom
and Jerry* fame.

"Flip the Frog" by Dean's, early 1930s, ht 20cm/8in, **£100–500**

▲ **"Flip the Frog" by Dean's**
Flip the Frog, created by Ub Iwerk and the star of MGM's *Fiddlestick* (1930), was highly popular in the early 1930s. This "Flip" was produced by Dean's Rag Book Co. in velvet and felt with a wire armature and plastic "googly" eyes. Comparatively rare in any condition, this "Flip" is virtually untouched and came in a plain card box in which he would have been delivered to the retailer. This explains the perfect condition and colour of the vulnerable felt feet and hands and the presence of the original swing tag and the Dean's printed mark on one foot.

"Lucky Jeep" by Dean's, c.1930, ht 18.5cm/7¼in, **£80–£300**

▲ **"Lucky Jeep" by Dean's**
The American cartoonist E.C. Segar introduced a character known as Eugene the Jeep into his *Popeye* cartoon strip in 1937. This "Lucky Jeep", so-called because of the printed four-leaf clovers on his velveteen body, was produced by Dean's (printed mark on foot) with a wire armature, a huge bulbous red nose and distinctive blue glass eyes. "Lucky Jeep" was not produced in large numbers and is therefore rarely found today; nevertheless, condition will still be crucial to value.

"March Hare" by Dean's, 1930s, ht 33cm/13in, **£100–500**

▲ **"March Hare" by Dean's**
In the 1930s Dean's produced an exceptionally high-quality set of characters from Lewis Carroll's *Alice in Wonderland* (1865) that included the "March Hare", the "White Rabbit", the "Dormouse" and "Alice" herself. Expensive at the time, these sets were not made in large quantities and are very rarely found today, although individual characters, such as the "March Hare" shown here, do appear. He is far better made than the average mass-produced toy, with a wire armature that allows him to be posed, wire-framed velvet ears, and a charming brushed cotton and felt outfit, all in very good condition.

"Wilfred", "Pip" and "Squeak",
1920s, ht of "Wilfred" 10cm/4in,
£80–200

▲ "Wilfred", "Pip" and "Squeak"

Wilfred (a baby rabbit), Pip (the dog) and Squeak (the penguin) were characters in a comic strip by A.B. Payne in the *Daily Mirror* from 1919 to 1953. The highly popular trio appeared in annuals, and fans could join the Wilfredian League of Gugnuncs (club memorabilia is also keenly collected). The soft-toy characters were made in a range of sizes. Although unmarked, this mohair pin-jointed set closely resembles the Farnell "Caesar" (see p.11). Like many miniatures the set is in very good condition, as tiny toys were less played with and often sold as mascots or adult novelty toys.

▼ Parrot

By an unknown maker, this parrot closely resembles Joey the Parrot, a character in *The Rainbow*, the first British comic exclusively for children that appeared from 1914 to 1956. The very soft body is rather simply and crudely modelled, with brushed cotton beak and feet that suggest an English maker. The mohair plush is slightly worn and grubby, and one eye is missing – this condition will be reflected in the value. Such a modestly priced toy could well appeal to a novice collector who might want to research the background and explore the possibilities of restoration.

Parrot, 1920s, ht 25.5cm/10in,
£40–150

▼ "Felix" by Schuco

Felix the Cat, created by the American animator Pat Sullivan c.1921, was one of the first famous cartoon characters and appeared in films, "the funnies", annuals and as merchandise. Although unmarked, this "Felix" has a metal, mohair-covered jointed frame and a printed metal clip-in face that identifies him as one of the highly popular Schuco miniatures (see p.31); in this case he has the added bonus of good condition.

"Felix" by Schuco, mid-1920s, ht 10cm/4in, **£100–300**

▼ English "Felix"

Felix appeared in a whole range of different styles, all keenly sought after by Felix collectors. The English versions tended to be quite skinny and slightly scary, with the distinctive teeth seen here in felt. This example is made of black-and-white mohair with a wire armature, and the tail is used as a tripod to keep him in the characteristic pose made famous by his signature tune: "Felix keeps on walking ... with his hands behind him".

English "Felix", 1920s, ht 35.5cm/14in, **£80–300**

▼ "Owl" by Agnes Brush

Although A.A. Milne's classics *Winnnie-the-Pooh* and *The House at Pooh Corner* were published in 1926 and 1928 respectively, all known soft-toy characters appeared in the 1950s (see p.51). This brushed-cotton "Owl", with orange felt eyes, beak and feet, is part of the range made by a small American manufacturer, Agnes Brush, whose swing-tag label is still in place. Agnes Brush toys were very much in the American craft soft rag-doll tradition; they were not made in large numbers and are rarely found in Europe.

"Owl" by Agnes Brush, 1950s, ht 25.5cm/10in, **£200–600**

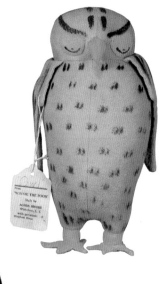

"Raggedy Arthur" by the Knickerbocker Toy Co.

Raggedy Arthur is a character from the classic American *Raggedy Ann Stories* by Johnny Gruelle, published in 1918. They were based on a rag doll found in the attic, and the family produced 200 dolls themselves before various manufacturers took over production. Like the American "Owl", this "Raggedy Arthur", made by the Knickerbocker Toy Co. in the 1960s, is typical of the rag-doll tradition, with a cotton body, sewn-and-applied features and woollen hair and will appeal primarily to American collectors.

"Raggedy Arthur" by the Knickerbocker Toy Co., 1960s, ht 30.5cm/12in, **£60–150**

"World Cup Willie"

Rather like the Olympic dachshund (see p.54), the "World Cup Willie" lion spans the soft toy/sports memorabilia collecting niches. The little British lion, made of synthetic plush and wearing a cotton Union Jack T-shirt, was produced in huge quantities for the 1966 World Cup. He is simply made, with embroidered features, and was inexpensive both when first made and now. Some 30 years old, he is just coming into the collecting market bracket and, modestly priced and with historical and sporting interest, might be a starting-point for a novice collector.

"World Cup Willie", 1966, ht 20cm/8in, **£8–15**

Eyes

Eyes can be a useful aid to dating and identifying unmarked toys, although remember that they have often been replaced, either by safety-conscious parents or through loss. Experience will teach you the different "feel" of wood, metal, glass (cold to touch or round edges) and plastic (warm to touch or sharp edges) eyes.
• Pre-World War I: boot-button eyes, wood, all sizes, solid colour (usually black; *see* p.10).
• Pre-World War I: glass eyes on some Steiff special-order toys.
• Pre- and post-World War I: plain metal and painted metal eyes (*see* p.43).
• Post-World War I: glass eyes introduced, either coloured or clear and painted on the back. "English" eyes: hand-painted on back (*see* p.35): "German" eyes: more uniform, almost "dipped" quality to painting on back.
• Pre-World War II: plastic "googly" eyes with loose pupil (*see* p.29).
• Post-World War II: plastic eyes more usual.
• Miniature toys have glass bead eyes.
• "Einco" and other early English toys have white glass eyes with applied coloured glass (*see* p.41).

FACT FILE

Birds

Unlike dogs, cats and rabbits, birds are not naturally "cuddly" animals and, with the exception of the fluffy chick – often produced as an Easter present – do not lend themselves easily to a soft-toy format. Nevertheless, most manufacturers did include them in their ranges and avoided the anatomical difficulties associated with realistic modelling, especially of the feet, by designing cuddly, comical or dressed versions, pull-along and mechanical toys and miniatures. As ever, Steiff led the way, producing cockerels and chickens as early as 1897. However, birds were in general consistently less popular – as they are now – and were hence produced in smaller quantities, which means that they are less readily found today.

Pull-along cockerel
by Steiff, c.1908,
ht 20cm/8in, **£300–800**

▶ **Pull-along cockerel by Steiff**
This cockerel has eccentric wooden wheels that give it a lifelike high-stepping gait. Its unjointed stuffed body is covered in layers of multi-coloured felt, still in amazingly unfaded condition, underneath which the Steiff button can be seen. Early felt toys are rarely found in such good condition, and this, together with its rarity, makes this toy highly attractive to collectors of both birds and Steiff toys.

▼ **"Pom-pom" miniatures by Steiff**
Steiff's tiny novelty pocket-money toys were launched in the 1930s. Animals with arms or legs, such as the Steiff donkey (see p.44), had wire frames covered with fine wool; birds were simple wool pom-poms. Pre-World War II birds were well made, with wire feet and legs and felt beaks and tail feathers; post-war birds have plastic feet and, sometimes, plastic beaks. Tiny bird boxes, branches and trees were sold as accessories and, although rarely found, can be a very effective way of displaying "Pom-pom" birds.

Pom-pom miniatures by Steiff,
1930s–50s, ht 2.5–5cm/1–2in,
pre-war **£20–80**; post-war **£5–30**

Duck by Bing, 1920s,
ht 20cm/8in, **£100–400**

▲ Duck by Bing

Gebrüder Bing was best-
known for its mechanical toys;
when wound through the hole
in its chest, this delightful
duck waddles along most
engagingly on its rigid metal
legs. Ideally, mechanical toys
should be in working
condition. Original keys
are nearly always
missing, as in this
example, but working
replacement keys –
often recycled clock
keys – can be
found. Both the
mechanism and the
mohair on this example
are in fine condition,
and the manufacturer's
name is stamped on
the metal surround of
the winding hole.

▼ "Hugo Crow" by Schuco

Manufacturers went to
great lengths to make
birds appealing, and "Hugo
Crow" is a good example of
how Schuco, well-known for its
original and comical fun toys
(see p.31), succeeded. Made
of mohair, with airbrushed
details, "Hugo", with his
exaggerated features (a huge
yellow felt beak, bright green
flat card-lined shoes, little
mohair topknot and typical
Schuco plastic eyes), has
abandoned any attempt at
realism in favour of charm.
Although unmarked, he
can be identified from the
Schuco catalogue as
an originally fairly
inexpensive toy,
whose comparative
rarity and good
condition add to
his appeal.

"Hugo Crow" by
Schuco, 1950s,
ht 18cm/7in,
£30–70

Wire armatures
• Well-known "bendy"
toys include Schuco's
"bigo-bello" range.
• Wire armatures were
sometimes used on
miniature toys (see p.50)
• Wire was used to
strengthen and pose
ears and tails (see p.10).
• "Pipe-cleaner" limbs
can be posed easily
(see p.52)
• Coiled springs were
used for "movement".

FACT FILE

"Kwacky-wack" by Einco, 1912,
ht 18cm/7in, **£80–250**

▲ "Kwacky-wack" by Einco

This early "Kwacky-wack" has
glass-painted eyes that can
be swivelled to change his
expression. The somewhat
clumsy modelling and
economical use of mohair
can also be seen on "Master
Bunny" (see p.24), and
"Kwacky-wack" has much the
same quirky appeal, in spite
of moth holes on his felt beak
and his replacement left foot.

Chick by Chiltern, post-1950s,
ht 10cm/4in, **£15–45**

Bird by Farnell, 1920s,
ht 20cm/8in, **£100–400**

▲ Bird by Farnell

This comic bird was made by
Farnell and designed by Chloë
Preston, a 1920s British
designer and illustrator, who
created the character for her
book *Peek-a-Boo Desert Island*.
Made of mohair and felt, with
a jointed head supporting a
fine piece of wire culminating
in a felt courtship feather, it is
extremely rare. This particular
example is unmarked and
was only identified when its
companion piece – a baby
bird called "Squawk-a-boo"
– was discovered with its
original label. The felt-backed
glass eyes are similar to those
used on Einco/Chiltern/Farnell
toys, and there was cross-
fertilization between the
companies, as skilled workers
often moved between them.

▲ Chick by Chiltern

Inexpensive and endearing
fluffy chicks were produced in
quantity for selling at Easter.
This post-war example, made
by Chiltern, has an unjointed
mohair body, felt beak and
legs and glass eyes. When first
produced it would have been
appealing but inexpensive
and unremarkable; today it
attracts interest because of
its immaculate, untouched
original condition. Part of an
unsold shop lot, it still has its
original ribbon and swing-tag
label and is a perfect example
of an inexpensive but popular
early post-war toy by a
leading British manufacturer.

Baby toy by Norah Wellings,
1930s, ht 33cm/13in, **£30–80**

▲ Baby toy by
Norah Wellings

Although better known for
her dolls, Norah Wellings'
small company also produced
a range of soft toys. This
engaging mohair bird, with
its huge felt beak and long
dangling wooden bead legs,
makes no concessions to
realistic modelling and was
designed to hang as a mobile
over a baby's cot or pram.
Marked with a label under the
left foot, it is an interesting
and rare example, in good
condition, of one of the
relatively few soft toys made
by a distinguished and
influential British designer.

Wire armatures: disadvantages
- Overbending can make the wire snap; restoration is possible.
- "Pipe cleaner" limbs are particularly easy to snap off and are therefore often missing.
- Broken wire can damage the body fabric: check carefully for tears or repairs.
- Rusty wire can stain badly and snaps quickly.

English duck, 1930s, ht 28cm/11in, **£40–150**

▲ English duck
Many of the smaller manufacturers did not label their toys, and this duck is without any identifying marks or labels. There are, however, several clues as to its origins: it is extremely well made of English mohair (see p.27), with airbrushed details, and although continental manufacturers also used English mohair, the fine modelling of the unjointed body is typically "English" and closely resembles that used on Farnell's "Jemima Puddleduck"; the spring in the neck was another feature found on English toys (see p.15).

"Belisha Beacon", c.1934, ht 30.5cm/12in, **£100–400**

▲ "Belisha Beacon"
Many novelty toys were commissioned for promotional purposes, often from smaller, less prestigious manufacturers, and were unmarked from the beginning. It seems highly likely that "Belisha Beacon" was commissioned as part of an educational programme on road safety for children. His simple stuffed mohair body has been ingeniously designed in the shape of the belisha beacons that are now increasingly being replaced in Great Britain by pelican crossing lights. This extremely rare toy by an unknown maker is in fair condition – the feet need attention – and is now valued as an amusing oddity.

Penguin, c.1920, ht 16.5cm/6½in, **£50–150**

▲ Penguin
This felt penguin, with its fixed clothes and little wooden sword, may well have been produced as a promotional toy. Although unmarked and unidentified (the only clue is the name "Orione" – probably that of a ship), it resembles Chiltern's pre-World War II dressed toys and has English painted metal eyes. Attribution would add to its value.

Farmyard animals

Farm animals, which feature so strongly in traditional nursery rhymes and action songs and games, are second only to household pets in terms of popularity with children and were made in large numbers by all manufacturers. As ever, Steiff led the way and began to produce farm animal toys alongside household pets as early as 1893. The earlier toys tended to be horses, ponies and donkeys, all ideally suited to the soft-toy format. Sheep, especially lambs, were also very popular, in particular as pull-along toys. Pigs are another favourite collecting niche and, perhaps under the influence of Beatrix Potter's *The Tale of Pigling Bland* and Disney's *Three Little Pigs* film, often appear dressed and in families.

▼ **Hobby horse by Steiff**
This hobby horse follows the traditional format of a horse's head mounted on a wooden pole with wheels. The head is very realistically modelled in mohair, with a horse-hair mane, glass eyes and an open felt mouth that would originally have held a bit and detachable leather bridle (now missing). Far fewer felt versions of this hobby horse have survived, as felt is so vulnerable to moth and hard to repair. Steiff hobby horses were made in different colours. Even if the ear button is missing, the wooden pole and wheels are often stamped with the company name.

Hobby horse by Steiff, 1920s, ht 114cm/45in, £80–300

▶ **"Pom-pom" donkey by Steiff**
"Pom-pom" miniatures were introduced by Steiff in the 1930s. These early "Pom-poms" are fine quality and now rare. This charming donkey is very simply made of fine wool. Less expensive and more readily found are the post-World War II "Pom-poms". All these animals were marked with Steiff buttons, which may now be missing; however, there are usually holes to indicate where they once were.

"Pom-pom" donkey by Steiff, 1930s, ht 13cm/5in, £30–120

▼ Bull by Chad Valley

Although cows were popular and produced in abundance, bulls were a different proposition, and this Chad Valley example has been given an airbrushed smiling mouth to make it less scary and more appealing. Rather crudely modelled, with an unjointed velvet body and stitched-on glass eyes, it is typical of many readily found unmarked middle-of-the-range toys. Fortunately this bull still has a red woven label on its belly – a bonus not only for the collector but also an aid to subsequent attribution of the many similar unmarked simple velvet toys.

Bull by Chad Valley, 1930s, l. 18cm/7in, **£40–150**

▼ Pig family

Pigs of any kind are a popular collecting niche, and this pig family, with the piglet still attached to the mother, is a good illustration of the move from realistic modelling to dressed pig-like rag dolls. Although unmarked they are probably English, but are difficult to date. The velvet heads are slightly worn and they have glass eyes; they are either good-quality post-war toys or slightly poorer quality pre-World War II toys.

Pig family, 1930s–40s, ht 35.5cm/14in, **£60–200**

Jointed toys

- Toys may be fully or partially jointed or unjointed; jointed toys are more desirable and highly priced.
- Fully jointed: head and limbs are constructed as separate parts and swivel independently (*see* squirrel, p.46)
- Partially jointed: only head and/or some limbs swivel (*see* fox, p.46)
- Unjointed: body constructed as one piece with fixed head and limbs (*see* bull below).

▼ French pull-along sheep

French soft toys are not very popular with collectors, even though French dolls are sought after worldwide. French makers used cheaper-quality materials and were in general less skilled at creating appealing animals. Although this sheep (unmarked but possibly by Fadap) has a rather forbidding expression, it is in virtually-unplayed-with condition, and the fixed felt limbs and ears and mohair coat are still remarkably clean.

French pull-along sheep, 1920s, l. 33cm/13in, **£100–300**

Woodland & field animals

The woodland and field soft toys found today were made both pre- and post-World War II. The more obviously appealing animals, such as foxes (influenced by fox hunting), deer, mice and squirrels, were made by most manufacturers; few, however, ventured into such traditionally unpopular and risky areas as insects and reptiles. The exception was, of course, Steiff, who in the 1950s and 1960s produced a limited range, often for a very short period due to lack of demand, that was made more saleable and appealing (and now more collectable) because the animals were given names. Although Steiff animals will always attract collectors, in general woodland and field animals are not a leading collecting area; they were produced in much smaller quantities and are now correspondingly rare.

"Fox" by Farnell,
1920s, ht
35.5cm/14in,
£80–300

▶ **"Fox" by Farnell**
The English manufacturer Farnell was enormously influenced by Steiff, and this fox attempts to emulate the German company's realistic modelling. Only the head, with its felt-backed glass eyes (metal eyes are also known), is jointed, so this fox remains in a fixed seated pose. The thick dense mohair, seen to particular advantage in the bushy tail, is of exceptional quality and still in excellent condition. Unmarked, it has been identified from previous labelled examples.

▼ **"Squirrel" by Steiff**
This lifelike red squirrel, which may have been influenced by Beatrix Potter's Squirrel Nutkin, is an early example of one of the more unusual of Steiff's animals. This toy is made of mohair, with glass eyes and horsehair whiskers. Fully jointed, the exceptionally good modelling has cleverly captured the alert pose and expression typical of the woodland squirrel. This example is, however, rather worn, especially on the nose and ears, which will inevitably lessen the value.

"Squirrel" by Steiff, c.1910,
ht 18cm/7in, **£100–400**

▼ Steiff creatures

The sheer quality of Steiff toys made even the most unappealing creatures engaging (see p.52). "Nelly the Snail", with a spotted velvet body, PVC shell and wax cloth underside, is now very rare; "Lizzy the Lizard" was also made of velvet. The rare "Spidy the Spider" has glass-bead eyes, and the small one has "pipe-cleaner" legs. "Wiggy the Weasel" is beautifully modelled in Dralon, with plastic whiskers, and has the added appeal of the original swing tag and Steiff ear button.

"Nelly the Snail", 1962–3, l. 10cm/4in, **£60–200**; "Lizzy the Lizard", 1959–62, l. 20cm/8in, 30.5cm/12in, **£20–100**; "Spidy the Spider", 1960–62, l. 12.5cm/ 5in and 23cm/9in, **£80–300**; "Wiggy the Weasel", post-1962, l. 12.5cm/5in, **£15–80**

"Fox cub" by Chad Valley, 1930s, ht 18cm/7in, **£60–200**

▲ "Fox cub" by Chad Valley

Many makers abandoned realism in favour of anthropomorphic appeal and produced dressed fox cubs, often in the form of a Little Red Riding Hood figure. This little doll-like mohair fox cub is unjointed and still retains her original felt outfit, including the rarely found detachable hat and card-lined shoes. The label on her foot indentifies her as pre-World War II.

Comical fieldmouse, late 1950s, ht 33cm/13in, **£40–120**

▲ Comical fieldmouse

This unmarked comical fieldmouse is typical of toys made in Italy or Spain in the late 1950s (see p.35). Although less sought after than German or English toys, this example is in good condition, complete with all its accessories. With its plastic eyes and moulded nose, nylon whiskers and airbrushed felt face (once green, now faded), it is a good example of its type.

Wild animals

A trip to the circus or the zoo was often one of the most memorable treats for young children, and an endearing soft-toy wild animal could rekindle the enjoyment and excitement of such a visit. The nearby Stuttgart zoo inspired many of the wild animals that were an important part of Steiff's earliest range, and by 1892 the company was producing 14 different types of elephant; it launched a highly successful "Circus" range *c.*1910. Other manufacturers followed Steiff's suit, and nearly all firms produced a variety of wild animals in many forms including realistically modelled, dressed, comical and pull-along and ride-on toys.

▼ **Steiff catalogue**
These pages from a 1950s catalogue give some idea of the range and variety of sizes of Steiff's wild animals. Members of the cat family were always popular, and lions could be bought as families, as shown here, with tiny cubs. Although a toy with a label, mark or swing tag will always be more sought after than one without, many unmarked animals can be successfully identified and attributed from catalogues. Steiff, in particular, has a comprehensive and impeccable archive collection.

Ride-on camel by Steiff, *c.*1900, l. 56cm/22in, **£300–1,200**

▲ **Ride-on camel by Steiff**
Pull-along and ride-on giraffes, lions and other animals were an early and enduring part of the Steiff range. This early camel has the distinctive Steiff modelling, together with a characteristic original red saddlecloth with gold braiding. It is in excellent condition; ride-on toys are often badly worn on top, and few examples have their original saddlecloths.

Steiff catalogue, 1950s, **£10–40**

"Paddy the Walrus" by Steiff, post-1959, ht 13cm/5in, **£20–60**

▲ **"Paddy the Walrus" by Steiff**
From the 1950s Steiff animals were given names – a shrewd marketing ploy that added to their appeal, especially with animals that were not inherently cuddly or appealing (see pp.52–3). This particular "Paddy" has lost his swing tag and button (usually found on the underside of the flipper) but he has been identified from the Steiff catalogue. Well designed, with stitched detail to his flippers, he is in excellent condition, with plastic eyes and tusks (which must be present for full value) and a brightly coloured, unworn, airbrushed mohair body.

▼ **"Mockie the Hippopotamus" and "Nosey the Rhinoceros" by Steiff**
Both "Nosey" and "Mockie" were part of the 1950s Steiff range and, typically, have airbrushed mohair bodies and plastic eyes. "Nosey's" horn and ears are felt, while "Mockie" has two square wooden teeth in his lower jaw. Although both have their buttons and tags, and "Nosey" still has his swing tag with his name, both could have been identified, if unmarked, from the catalogue opposite, where they appear on the top right-hand page.

"Mockie the Hippopotamus", post-1954, ht 13cm/5in, **£70–120**; "Nosey the Rhinoceros", post-1954, ht 13cm/5in, **£70–120**

Ride-on elephant by Steiff, 1950s, ht 89cm/35in, **£80–400**

▲ **Ride-on elephant by Steiff**
Elephants have featured in the Steiff range from day one (see p.56). The worn back of this giant mohair elephant is typical of a well-loved toy, but it still has a working pull-cord voice and felt tusks. First launched in 1914, ride-on elephants are still being made, although more recent ones have thicker rubber tyres than those on the blue-painted metal ones seen here.

▼ Elephant by Farnell

The Farnell mohair elephant shown here, inspired by Steiff and clearly labelled on the left foot, is a cuddly rather than a realistic animal, and the cotton body tells us that it would originally have been dressed. Missing or replacement clothes will reduce the value, in spite of otherwise excellent condition, as in this case. A similar elephant wearing a green felt suit is known, and it is possible that this elephant may have originally had a similar suit, perhaps inspired by Babar, the elephant hero of the books published by Jean de Brunhoff from 1931.

Elephant by Farnell, 1930s,
ht 25.5cm/10in, **£80–200**
(undressed), **£100–400** (dressed)

▼ Elephant by Schuco

This little jointed elephant, with felt ears and tusks, is part of the Schuco "yes/no" mechanism range made in the 1950s. The mechanism is operated by the tail, which has often lost its mohair covering, as here, even though the rest of the metal-frame mohair-covered body may be in excellent condition. Other manufacturers copied the "yes/no" mechanism, but, although unmarked, this particular elephant has the distinctive Schuco plastic eyes as a further aid to attribution.

Elephant by Schuco, 1950s,
ht 10cm/4in, **£60–200**

▼ "Noah's Ark" lion by Schuco

Miniatures are very popular with collectors because they are so easy to display and relatively inexpensive. This miniature lion is part of the Schuco "Noah's Ark" range and came in a distinctive original box, which, if present, will add to appeal and value. The tiny wire frame is fully jointed, with the characteristic rubber neck. Although produced as inexpensive novelty toys, "Noah's Ark" animals are very well made and sought after today. Lions are the most common; the poodle (see p.13) is rare.

"Noah's Ark" lion by Schuco,
1950s, ht 7.5cm/3in, **£40–80**

"Toto-Twiga" and "Honey Boy" by Woolnough

"Toto-Twiga", a baby giraffe, and "Honey Boy", a bear cub, were characters from an American story book by Osa Johnson and were produced as soft toys in the early 1920s by F.W. Woolnough Co. Inc. All Johnson animals, which are excellent copies of the illustrations, are extremely rare. Although unmarked, they are good examples of high-quality original toys that have been subsequently identified from popular children's books, and this particular "Honey Boy" and "Toto-Twiga" were accompanied by a copy of the book.

"Toto-Twiga" and "Honey Boy" by Woolnough, 1920s;
"Toto-Twiga" ht 30.5cm/12in;
"Honey Boy" l. 28cm/11in;
£150–400 (each)

"Kanga" and "Roo" by Merrythought

The story of Christopher Robin and his friends inspired many soft toys, but this "Kanga" and "Roo" were based on the characters from the Disney film (1967) and were produced under licence, together with other Milne characters, by Merrythought from 1967 to 1976. "Roo" is often missing, and collectors will pay quite highly to find a single joey or "Roo" to pop into "Kanga's" pouch. This unjointed mohair "Kanga" is in good condition and has her printed label.

"Kanga" and "Roo" by Merrythought, 1966–76, ht 35.5cm/14in, **£30–120**

Winnie-the-Pooh

A.A. Milne based his books *Winnie-the-Pooh* (1926) and *The House at Pooh Corner* (1928) on his son's soft toys (*see* p.7), now housed in New York. The original Pooh was a Farnell bear; Piglet and Eeyore – unmarked English toys – were presents from neighbours, while Kanga, Roo and Tigger were later additions. There was little merchandizing until after the Disney films (1967 and 1968).

Lioness by Steiff

Steiff made huge numbers of lions in a range of sizes, both as individuals and in sets, as unjointed reclining or seated toys, or as more expensive jointed versions. This jointed lioness is in excellent condition and has an unusual hand-embroidered red-and-black nose. It is a good example of an early post-war Steiff toy, which would be readily found and therefore more reasonably priced than rare examples – a good buy for a novice collector who may have a limited budget.

Lioness by Steiff, 1950s, l. 20cm/8in, **£20–80**

Oddities

Fierce competition between manufacturers led to the production of ever more bizarre and inventive soft toys in an attempt to generate sales and expand the market. Almost every company wanted to produce that "something different", and insects, monsters and other wild flights of imagination appeared, together with toys that "could do something". Many items found their way into novelty shops; less successful lines were only produced for short periods of time. As a result, oddities are comparatively rare and not generally avidly collected. The exception, as always, tends to be Steiff, whose oddities have the appeal of fine modelling and quality production if not of conventional charm.

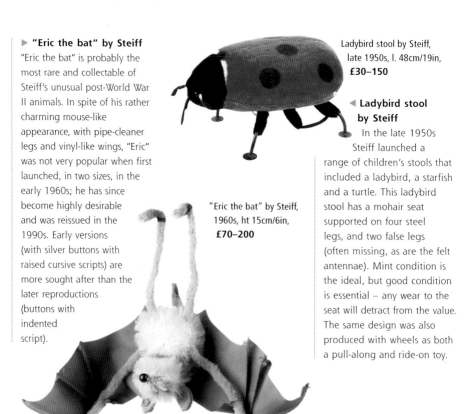

▶ **"Eric the bat" by Steiff**
"Eric the bat" is probably the most rare and collectable of Steiff's unusual post-World War II animals. In spite of his rather charming mouse-like appearance, with pipe-cleaner legs and vinyl-like wings, "Eric" was not very popular when first launched, in two sizes, in the early 1960s; he has since become highly desirable and was reissued in the 1990s. Early versions (with silver buttons with raised cursive scripts) are more sought after than the later reproductions (buttons with indented script).

Ladybird stool by Steiff, late 1950s, l. 48cm/19in, **£30–150**

"Eric the bat" by Steiff, 1960s, ht 15cm/6in, **£70–200**

◀ **Ladybird stool by Steiff**
In the late 1950s Steiff launched a range of children's stools that included a ladybird, a starfish and a turtle. This ladybird stool has a mohair seat supported on four steel legs, and two false legs (often missing, as are the felt antennae). Mint condition is the ideal, but good condition is essential – any wear to the seat will detract from the value. The same design was also produced with wheels as both a pull-along and ride-on toy.

"Dino the Dinosaur" by Steiff, late 1950s, l. 46cm/18in, **£80–400**

Marks
Manufacturers used a variety of marks:
- Woven cloth labels: sewn into seams, the undersides of the feet or some other discreet site.
- Printed marks: around the necks, under the feet or undersides of toys.
- Paper or card tags: often removed, but there may be remnants of cotton stitches.
- Metal buttons: these leave holes if lost – holes are sometimes faked.
- Swing tags: on threads.
- Metal-rimmed labels.

▼ **"Crabby the lobster" by Steiff**

"Crabby the lobster" was launched in the early 1960s in three sizes (10cm/4in; 18cm/7in and 28cm/11in). Although beautifully modelled in felt and mohair, with fine airbrushed detail and pipe-cleaner legs, lobsters would not have had a universal appeal for young children, and "Crabby" perhaps remained essentially more of an adult novelty toy. The original tag (clearly visible on the larger "Crabby") and the Steiff button on the leg, together with good condition and bright colour, add to the appeal.

"Crabby the lobster" by Steiff, early 1960s, l. 10cm/4in and 28cm/11in, **£30–150**

▲ **"Dino the dinosaur" by Steiff**

The late 20thC craze for and interest in dinosaurs among young children did not extend to the soft-toy market, and the various types of dinosaur that Steiff produced in a range of sizes (including a giant two-metre-long studio version) did not sell well and are now very rare. The original airbrushed designs were very brightly coloured in purples, greens and blues; this "Dino" is slightly faded, which will reduce his value, but he still has the Steiff button on one of his spikes.

English monster, 1920s/1930s, ht 15cm/6in, **£20–80**

▼ **English monster**

This strange soft stuffed monster is a mystery. The eccentric head has a fur trim that continues along the spine, the purple-and-yellow velvet body is rather faded, and the head is distinctly floppy. The larger boot-button eye is a replacement. Although it is unmarked, the materials and style suggest that it was made by an English manufacturer, and it is a good example of an early oddity that now has a distinct forlorn charm.

"Olympia Waldi", 1972,
l. 25.5cm/10in, **£5–15**

▲ **"Olympia Waldi"**
Many soft toys were
produced as versions
of sports mascots and
memorabilia. This particular
dachshund – "Olympia Waldi"
– was the mascot of the
Munich Olympics of 1972,
and the 1970s influence is
clearly visible in his brightly
coloured striped cotton body.
Stuffed toys made in the
1960s, 1970s and 1980s are
generally inexpensive, readily
available and, at present,
not very sought after, but
examples such as this, with a
particular historical interest,
may well prove a useful long-
term investment for a novice
collector with limited funds.

"Bumblebees", left: 1920s,
ht 33cm/13in, **£60–150**;
right: c.1915, ht 33cm/13in,
£60–150

▲ **"Bumblebees"**
Although made by different
manufacturers – one English,
one from New Zealand –
these strange "bumblebees"
with their black-and-orange
mohair bodies, wire armatures
and stiffened net wings are
clearly based on the same
design. The earlier "bee"
(right), with brightly coloured
felt hands and a clean velvet
face and made by Ealon Toys,
is in excellent condition; the
later "bee" (left), by Luvmee
Toys of New Zealand, is
slightly more worn and
grubby but has an engaging
expression. Unusually, both
have their original swing tags.

Tortoise, 1930s, ht 36cm/14in,
£60–200

▲ **Tortoise**
Italian and Spanish
manufacturers made a
wide range of felt soft toys,
including tourist souvenirs.
This comical but well-made
example is sculpted in felt,
with no movement but has
plenty of detail in its unusual
felt walking outfit, complete
with felt shoes and hat.
Unmarked, it was probably
made by a small-scale maker
and is an interesting example
of a fairly rare continental
post-war felt toy in excellent
condition (see also p.35).

Post-World War II toys
- Generally less well made (Steiff is the exception to this rule).
- Increasing use of man-made fibres such as Dralon, PVC, vinyl and cotton, sometimes in conjunction with mohair.
- Increasing use of plastic eyes (*see* p.39) and noses, and nylon whiskers.
- Increasing use of washable foam stuffing.
- Good starting-point for novice collectors.

Parrot teacosy, 1930s, ht 29cm/11½in, **£30–90**

Hat stand, 1920s/1930s, ht 33cm/13in, **£20–80**

▲ Hat stand
In the 1920s there was a vogue for novelty hat stands, and this English example has substituted a mohair dog's head, with a stitched mouth and nose and bright orange glass eyes, for the more readily found "flapper's" head. Although unusual, it is not very valuable; the head is worn, the pink paint on the wooden stand is flaking, and a disembodied animal head may have limited appeal. Nevertheless, it is an interesting example of a very English Art Deco novelty that would appeal equally to collectors of soft toys, of curios and of Art Deco.

▲ Parrot teacosy
Soft toys were incorporated into a variety of household objects, including pot holders (see p.27), miniature egg cosies (often chickens) and tea cosies, as seen here. This cosy is made of very good quality artificial silk plush, fully lined and padded; the parrot has a flat body with felt feet, a three-dimensional stuffed head with glass eyes and a felt beak that acts as a handle. Although unmarked, this novelty tea cosy, which was also produced with a monkey, is quintessentially English.

"Bertha the Siberian Cheesehound" by Steiff, 1927, ht 23cm/9in, **£500–3,000**

▲ "Bertha the Siberian Cheesehound" by Steiff
Rube Goldberg, who produced the "Boob McNutt" Sunday comic series from 1915 until 1934, created "Bertha the Siberian Cheesehound". Steiff was commissioned to produce just 24 "Berthas", in two sizes (18cm/7in and 23cm/9in), which are now extremely rare. This example, from the Steiff archive, has a fully jointed mohair body and felt face.

Steiff

Fired by the success of the Steiff teddy bear, every collector wants to own a Steiff soft toy. Founded by a remarkable woman – Margarete Steiff – in Giengen, southern Germany, the company was probably the first, and is certainly the most successful and most prestigious, of all soft-toy manufacturers. The first catalogue appeared in 1893, and Steiff toys, famous for their innovatory designs, fine modelling, attention to detail and superb quality, have been considered the Rolls-Royces of the trade ever since. Steiff was years ahead of its time in terms of quality control, marketing skills, punctilious marking, archive material and readiness to sue for any infringement of its registered designs. Few collectors can afford the rare and highly sought-after pre-World War I toys, but post-World War II animals are more readily found and more reasonably priced.

"Teddy Girl" by Steiff, 1905, ht 46cm/18in, sold for **£110,000**

◀ **"Teddy Girl"**
Steiff teddy bears are now a serious investment area, and "Teddy Girl" is the famous bear who was sold for £110,000 at Christie's, London, in December 1994. A rare cinnamon, mohair bear and much admired in her own right, she was the lifelong companion of the late Colonel Bob Henderson, one of the first teddy-bear collectors, who had photographs of himself with his beloved bear from childhood onwards. This charming provenance contributed to the record price paid for the world's most expensive teddy bear/soft toy.

▼ **The beginning**
This felt elephant pincushion, now in the Steiff archives, is a fascinating example of the small animal that launched Steiff and also featured on its first button. The pincushion was made in 1880 by Margarete Steiff as a present for her sister-in-law Ann, whose initials are marked on the toy. It was the success of these homemade presents that encouraged a young, wheelchair-bound seamstress to start the world-famous soft-toy company.

Pincushion, 1880, ht 10cm/4in, **unable to value**

▼ Range and diversity

The range and diversity of Steiff designs were always exceptional, and where Steiff led, other manufacturers often followed. Early (and now very rare) sets of skittles, made from 1892, were joined by "Roly Poly" toys (see p.22), pull-along and ride-on toys. Steiff was the first company to spot the potential of such characters as Peter Rabbit, applied for licences for Disney toys (see p.32) and other comic characters (see p.34), and in the 1950s launched a highly unusual range of creatures (see pp.52–3), made endearing by clever marketing and superb Steiff modelling.

Skittles, 1904, ht of bear king pin 25.5cm/10in, set sold for **£4,500**

"Scotty", 1920s, ht 11.5cm/4½in, sold for **£1,500**

▲ Marks and condition

This black mohair "Scottie dog" is every collector's dream. Steiff went to great lengths to mark its toys, and this little trade sample dog has a profusion of marks, all intact: a Steiff ear button with a crisp label, an immaculate swing tag with its name – "Scotty" – a further tag on the original leather collar, and, around the tail, a label with a recommended retail price. The dog is also in exceptional, mint condition – the perfect collector's toy.

▼ Provenance

This charming photograph shows a little English girl proudly clasping her much loved Steiff "Peter Rabbit", who, when he reached the saleroom, was rather worn and wearing a replacement felt jacket and homemade slippers. Just like "Teddy Girl", this toy had also been a lifelong friend.

"Peter Rabbit", c.1912, ht 20cm/8in, photo and rabbit sold for **£1,100**

Manufacturers

Agnes Brush (est. USA; earliest recorded toys produced 1930s)
Swing card tag with company name

Alpha Toys see J.K. Farnell

Berg (est. Fieberbrunn, Austria, post-World War II)
Plain, red, metal-and-enamel heart

Bing, Gebrüder (est. Nuremberg, 1865, by Ignaz and Adolf Bing; production ceased 1932)

Metal arrows (pre-World War I)

Circular tags (post-World War I)

Chad Valley (est. as Chad Valley, Birmingham, 1897; taken over by Palitoy 1978)
1920s and 1930s: label (as below), embroidered in red; usually on foot

HYGIENIC TOYS
MADE IN ENGLAND BY
CHAD VALLEY Cº Lᵀᵉ

Chiltern Toys (est. as Chiltern Toys, Chesham, 1924; taken over by Chad Valley 1967)
Label printed "Chiltern Hygienic Toys Made in England"

Dean's Rag Book Co.
(est. London, 1903, by Samuel Dean; still in production)
Printed name, usually around neck, or underneath foot; swing tags; printed labels

MADE IN GREAT BRITAIN
BY DEANS RAG BOOK CO. LTD.

Ealon Toys (est. as East London Toy Factory, 1914; production ceased early 1950s)
Label with woven name

Einco see Eisenmann & Co.

Eisenmann & Co. (est. Fuerth, Bavaria, and London, 1881, by Joseph and Gabriel Eisenmann)
Major importer and distributor using "Kiddieland" and "Einco" trademarks; metal-rimmed, circular name tag

Fadap (est. as Fabrique artistique d'animaux en peluche, Divonne-les-Brins, 1920s; ceased production in the 1970s)
White, circular swing tag

Isaac & Co. (Isa Toy)
(est. London, 1881; taken over by Chad Valley, 1923)
Label with woven lettering "Isa Toys"

J.K. Farnell (est. as silk merchants, London, c.1840, by John Kirby Farnell; relocated Hastings, 1959; bought by finance firm, 1968; relaunched through Merrythought, 1996)

Paper tags (until 1925)

Circular tags (until 1925)

Embroidered labels (1925–45)

JOPI see Pitrmann, Josef

Kersa see Walter, W. KG

Knickerbocker Toy Co. (est. New York, 1924; still in production)

Printed labels

Luvmee (est. New Zealand; earliest recorded toy made 1939; production probably started earlier) Tag and label

Merrythought Ltd (est. Ironbridge, Shropshire, 1930: still in production)

Embroidered labels (pre-World War I)

Printed labels (post-World War II)

Metal buttons used pre-World War II

Norah Wellings (est. Wellington, Shropshire, 1926; closed 1959)

MADE IN ENGLAND
BY
NORAH WELLINGS

Label with embroidered name

Pitrmann, Josef (est. Nuremberg, 1910; JoPi trademark registered 1921; closed 1959) Swing tags

Pixie Toys (est. England, early 1930s; closed 1962) Label with woven name

Schreyer & Co. (est. Nuremberg, 1912, by Heinrich Muller and Heinrich Schreyer; ceased production 1976) Swing tags

Schuco see Schreyer & Co.

Steiff, Margarete GmbH (est. Giengen, 1877; still in production) Buttons, cloth labels and tags all used; see *Button in Ear* for further details

Elephant button (1904–5)

Blank button (1905–9 and 1948–50)

Pre-war button (early1920s–1950)

Post-war button (1952–70)

Chest label for "Bully" by Steiff (1928–1950)

Walter, W. KG (est. Lobositz, nr Prague, by W. Walter, 1920; relocated to Mindelheim, Germany, 1948; closed, 1956) Swing tags

Wendy Boston (est. nr Abergavenny, Glamorgan, by Wendy Boston, 1945; ceased production, 1976) Label with printed name

Woolnough, F.W. & Co. (est. New York; publishing company, only known toys dated 1920s) Toys unmarked and identified only from accompanying children's book

Care & restoration

Moth damage

Soft toys are vulnerable to insects, damp, dirt and direct sunlight. The smell of mothballs can be overpowering, and a more environmentally friendly and pleasant alternative to keep your toys safe from moth damage is a small toy-shaped homemade bag filled with lavender, which can be tucked into a group of toys quite unobtrusively. One way of ensuring that a new addition to your collection is moth-free is to place it inside two double-sealed plastic bags and put it into the deep freeze overnight.

Handling, display, cleaning and sunlight

Constant handling leads to wear, so display your toys on a shelf or chair where they do not have to be moved on a daily basis. Although some post-World War II toys are washable, cleaning early toys and those made from natural fibres is more difficult. The golden rule is to use the absolute minimum of everything and not to wet the fabric or stuffing. Toys should never be dry cleaned. Mohair can be combed gently with a wide-toothed comb that will not break or pull the fabric and then gently sponged or wiped down with the lather only from a proprietary "soft wash" soap product – never use detergent. Artificial-silk-plush, felt and velvet toys are more problematic to clean; however, although they should never be made wet, some dirt can be removed from them by gentle brushing with a fine baby's toothbrush. Direct sunlight fades colour – felt toys or clothes are particularly vulnerable. Temperature range is not usually a problem, provided that you avoid extremes, but damp can rot stuffing, particularly if it is made from wood wool.

Restoration

The golden rules with restoration are never do anything that cannot be undone, and, if in any doubt about what you are doing or whether restoration can or should be carried out, always seek the advice of a professional restorer. However, simple restoration and repair can be carried out at home, and it can be enormously satisfying to bring a toy back to life through careful cleaning and repair.

Wear, tear and holes

Wear cannot be restored, and holes will need to be looked at by a professional. However, bald spots can be carefully covered with clothes, split seams can be repaired with appropriate thread, loose ears or tails can be sewn back on, and missing ears can often be replaced by splitting remaining double ears. Leave worn paw pads in place and either re-cover or back holes.

Replacement parts, sewing and re-dressing

Antique-toy fairs and antiques dealers can be a useful source of replacement eyes, noses and "spare parts". Sewn facial features such as noses and mouths need very sensitive treatment; the face and expression are usually what gives the toy its particular appeal, so try to find books or catalogues to make sure that the restoration is accurate, and, if in any doubt, consult a professional. Any re-dressing should be in keeping with the original clothes – again, books and catalogues will help you to determine what clothes would be most appropriate to your particular toy. Moth damage on existing clothes cannot be concealed, but holes in felt clothes can be filled by placing new felt under the existing garments.

Glossary

Armature, wire Support made of wire around which a toy is constructed

Artificial silk plush Manmade warp-pile fabric used to imitate mohair

Boot-button eyes Solid wooden eyes with metal loops on back

Burlap Coarse, canvas-like cloth

Composition Substance made from wood or paper pulp, reinforced with other ingredients such as rags, bones, eggs, wood or plastic

Disc joints Wooden or cardboard discs placed betweeen the limbs and torso that allow smooth and full movement of the limbs

Dralon/Draylon Acrylic fibre used in post-World War II toys

Eccentric wheels Wheels with a non-central axle that turn unevenly

Excelsior see wood wool

Felt Soft fabric formed from matting, rather than weaving, wool fibres

"Googly" eyes Round plastic eyes with pupils that move

Growler Internal voice box that produces a growl

Kapok Very light, soft fibre from tropical tree used for stuffing

Mohair Long, soft hair from Angora goat

Patent Official document to protect a new invention

Pin joints Limbs joined to the torso by a pin

Plush Natural fabric with long, open pile

Provenance Documented history

Pull-cord voice Voice-box activated by a pull-cord

Squeaker Voice-box activated by squeezing a toy (by hand pressure)

Stockinette Knitted cotton/ elastic fabric

String joints Early type of joint, joined to the torso by string

Unjointed toy Toy in which both torso and limbs are formed in one piece

Velvet Fabric, usually silk or cotton, with soft close-cut pile

Velveteen Cotton or mixed cotton and silk fabric, similar to velvet

Vinyl Non-flammable, flexible form of plastic

Voice-box Internal mechanical device used to produce a sound and activated by squeezing or tipping a toy

Wood wool Long, thin wood shavings used for stuffing toys; also known as excelsior

What to read

BOOKS

Axe, J. The Magic of Merrythought (Hobby Horse, 1986; 2nd ed. Merrythought, 1998)

Beckett, Alison Miller's Collecting Teddy Bears & Dolls: The Facts At Your Fingertips (Mitchell Beazley, 1996)

Cieslik, J. and M. Button in Ear: The History of the Teddy Bear and his Friends (Marianne Cieslik Verlag, 1989)

Hillier, M. (ed) Pollock's Dictionary of English Dolls (Robert Hale, 1982)

Hockenberry, D. Enchanted Friends (Schiffer, 1995)

Maniera, Leyla The Christie's World of Teddy Bears (Christie's, 2000)

Pistorious, R. and C. Steiff Sensational Teddy Bears, Animals and Dolls (Hobby House, 1990)

UK Teddy Bear Guide (Hugglets, published annually)

Where to see and buy

Soft toys, as opposed to teddy bears, are still a relatively new collecting area, and, as yet, few museums have extensive collections and there are relatively few specialist dealers or auctions. Doll, teddy-bear and antiques fairs are regular events in Britain and other countries – check specialist magazines and local advertisements for venues; charity shops and car-boot sales can also be a rich source of soft toys. The *UK Teddy Bear Guide* (published annually by Hugglets) is an invaluable comprehensive guide and lists dealers, museums, shops, fairs and restorers; the addresses below are only intended as a starting-point.

COLLECTIONS

Basel Museum
Puppenhausmuseum
Steinenvorstadt 1
CH-4051 Basel, Switzerland

**Bethnal Green Museum
of Childhood**
Cambridge Heath Road
London E2 9PA, UK

Merrythought Museum
The Wharfage
Ironbridge TF8 7NJ
Shropshire, UK

Museum of Childhood
42 High St
Edinburgh EH1 1TG, UK

Steiff Archive Museum
Margarete Steiff GmbH
Giengen, Germany
(Steiff's extensive archive
is not open to the public)

SPECIALIST DEALERS
Barbara Baldwin
Old Friends Antiques
PO Box 754
Sparks, MD 21152, USA

Jane Drummond
Hope Cottage
Cottwood
Riddlecombe
Devon EX18 7PG, UK

Pam Hebbs
The Teddy Bear Shop
5 The Annexe
Camden Passage
London N1 8EU, UK

Dee Hockenberry
Bears N' Things
14191 Bacon Road
Albion, NY 14411, USA

Sue Pearson
13 Prince Albert Street
The Lanes
Brighton
East Sussex BN1 1HE, UK

Teddy Bears of Witney
99 High Street
Witney OX8 6LY, UK

MAJOR AUCTION HOUSES
Bonhams Chelsea
65–9 Lots Road
London SW10 0RN, UK

Butterfield & Butterfield
220 San Bruno Avenue
San Francisco CA 94103, USA

Christie's South Kensington
85 Old Brompton Road
London SW7 3LD, UK

Christie's
502 Park Avenue
New York NY 10021, USA

Christie's East
219 East 67th Street
New York NY 10021, USA

Phillips Bayswater
10 Salem Road
London W2 4DI, UK

Skinner Inc.
357 Main Street
Bolton MA 01740, USA

Sotheby's
34–5 New Bond Street
London W1A 2AA, UK

Sotheby's
1334 York Avenue
New York NY 10021, USA

Index

Acknowledgments

The consultants would like to say special thanks to: Margarete Steiff GmbH, for the loan of unique material from its archive; Merrythought; Dee Hockenberry; Debbie Strutt, for photography; and a personal thank you to Pam Hebbs, a dear friend. The publishers would like to thank Laura Hicks, Claire Musters and Amanda Patton (illustrator) for their invaluable help in the preparation of this book.

Jacket photograph and picture p.2 by Steve Tanner © Octopus Publishing Group Ltd. Toys supplied courtesy of Leyla Maniera and Daniel Agnew. All other pictures courtesy of Leyla Maniera and Daniel Agnew except: 10t, 10b, 16t, 17tr, 17br, 19r, 22r, 23bl, 23tc, 27bl, 30l, 30r, 31tl, 32l, 35tl, 36tl, 38c, 40l, 51bl, 54c, 55c, 56l, 57l, 57c, 57r Christie's South Kensington; 32b, 32,t, 33 Christie's South Kensington/Disney characters © Disney Enterprises, Inc. Used by permission from Disney Enterprises, Inc.; 38r, 39l Dee Hockenberry; 7 From the collections of the Central Children's Room, Donnell Library Center, The New York Public Library; 9t © Leyla Maniera and Daniel Agnew/Picture reproduced courtesy of Hamleys; 8, 23r, 34l, 34r, 56r Steiff; 55r Steiff/Picture courtesy of Steiff, after an original sketch by R.C. Goldberg. Key: t: top, b: bottom, c: centre, l: left, r: right.